The Traveling Tree

The Traveling Tree

Lessons from a Nomadic Life

Michio Hoshino

Translated by Eli K. P. William

Originally published in Japan in 1995 as
TABI WO SURU KI by Bungeishunju Ltd., Tokyo.

First published in Great Britain in 2025 by Gaia, an imprint of
Octopus Publishing Group Ltd
Carmelite House
50 Victoria Embankment
London EC4Y 0DZ
www.octopusbooks.co.uk
www.octopusbooksusa.com

An Hachette UK Company
www.hachette.co.uk

The authorized representative in the EEA is Hachette Ireland,
8 Castlecourt Centre, Dublin 15, D15 XTP3, Ireland (email: info@hbgi.ie)

TABI WO SURU KI by Michio Hoshino Copyright © 1995 Naoko Hoshino.
All rights reserved. Original Japanese edition published by Bungeishunju Ltd.,
in 1995. English translation rights reserved by OCTOPUS PUBLISHING GROUP,
under the license granted by Naoko Hoshino, arranged with Bungeishunju Ltd.,
through Japan UNI Agency, Inc. and Vicki Satlow of The Agency.

Translation copyright © 2025 Eli K. P. William

Distributed in the US by Hachette Book Group
1290 Avenue of the Americas, 4th and 5th Floors
New York, NY 10104

Distributed in Canada by Canadian Manda Group
664 Annette St., Toronto, Ontario, Canada M6S 2C8

ISBN: 978-1-85675-590-0
eISBN: 978-1-85675-592-4

A CIP catalogue record for this book is available from the British Library.

Typeset in 10.75/16.5pt Farnham Text by Six Red Marbles UK, Thetford, Norfolk.

Printed and bound in India by Manipal Technologies Limited

3 5 7 9 10 8 6 4 2

Commissioning Editor: Jessica Minocha
Editor: Scarlet Furness
Copy Editor: Monica Hope
Creative Director: Mel Four
Production Controller: Sarah Parry

This FSC® label means that materials used for
the product have been responsibly sourced.

Contents

CONTENTS

Note on the Translation

The essays in this volume were all written between 1993 and 1995 when understanding of indigenous cultures was different than it is today. In order for the text to be accessible to the widest possible audience, some cultural terms that appear in the original text reflect current usage. We hope that these alterations are the minimum sufficient for a wide range of readers to enjoy these essays while remaining as sincere to the author's vision as possible.

PART ONE

A New Voyage

The season of fresh spring green is over in Fairbanks and early summer is approaching.

I'm gathering dry branches in the twilight to make a fire out front when I hear from this way and that the calls of red squirrels. Droppings left by a moose in winter remain on the soft carpet of the forest floor now clear of snow, and I wonder when that enormous creature could have passed by our house unbeknown to us.

The silvery caress of the breeze on my cheek is another sign of the change all around. Even after fifteen years living in Alaska, I still love how the seasons in this land shift distinctly from one to the next like the pages of a book turning.

Human emotion is such a funny thing. We are swayed by the most insignificant daily trifles. And yet the touch of a breeze or the hint of a nascent summer can bring us such fulfillment. Our minds are both deep and strangely shallow. Only within that shallowness are we able to go on living.

Now that I'm married and beginning anew, other kinds of change are afoot. As I was tidying up my old belongings a few days ago, I found something that really brought me back. My diary from 1978, the year I moved to Alaska.

When I opened the time-weathered notebook to the first page, a powerful sense of nostalgia welled up in me as though I had come face to face with a version of myself from long ago. I had written the inaugural entry inside the cabin of a plane that had just taken off from Narita Airport bound for Alaska. One passage in particular, a sort of declaration of my intentions, brought a wistful smile to my face. How excited I must have been to have jotted down such a thing. As embarrassing as the passage was to read all these years later, it offered a sincere portrait of who I was then, on the verge of stepping into the unknown. Taking a break from my cleanup, I lost myself for a time in this old record of my youth.

In those days, I just couldn't get my mind off Alaska. As though delirious with fever, going there was all I could think about. I had no choice but to set sail mapless and without compass.

Upon arrival at the airport in Fairbanks, I headed straight to the University of Alaska. I was determined to enroll in the Department of Biology and Wildlife. But when I submitted my documents to the office of admissions, it turned out that I was some thirty points shy of the English score required for international students; they told me, in short, that it would be impossible to admit me that year. Still, I wasn't about to just return to Japan. My yearning for Alaska was fully mature; my ship had already pushed off.

So I went to see the chair of the department. He had known I would be flying over from Japan as I had sent him several letters. I could hardly speak the English language, but I nevertheless made a desperate effort to explain my feelings. How I wanted to take my time coming to grips with the Arctic wilderness. How the only way I could do that was by getting into his department. How I couldn't write off a whole year because of a mere thirty points . . . and how I had long dreamed of living in Alaska.

The list of reasons I gave seems so absurd in retrospect – and to a department chair who I had only met for the first time! What did my personal desires matter to a university? But in my panic at that moment, it was the university's policy excluding admission over a few trivial points that seemed absurd.

The department chair sat quietly listening to my plea. Then, with a slight smile, said, 'Got it. In that case, we'll let you into the university on my authority. I'm going to call admissions, so please go there now.'

I felt as though I had ascended to the heavens. Unable to contain myself, I quickly gave up on walking and started to run through the campus. From my vantage on the hill upon which the university stands, the peaks and glaciers of the Alaska Range stretched distinctly along the distant horizon. I couldn't help feeling that the chain of mountains was calling to me. It was that time of year when the soft breeze of early summer has begun to blow – just as it is blowing right now.

I came to Alaska bearing numerous dreams and began to travel across the land as if to digest them one by one. Atop the blank map that was Alaska, I had to draw the map of myself.

I hiked the pristine mountains and valleys of the Brooks Range that cut across the Arctic reaches of the state. I voyaged by kayak through Glacier Bay, listening to the primeval groan of glaciers. I rowed a seal-skin *umiak* with Inuit to hunt right whales in the Arctic Ocean. I witnessed a magical potlatch festival at an Athabascan village. I followed the caribou on their intrepid journeys, enthralled by their seasonal migrations. I gazed up at countless northern lights and came across countless wolves. Most illuminating of all, I met all sorts of people and came to know many different ways of life. . . . And before I knew it, fifteen years had gone by.

My own map of Alaska has gradually revealed itself. Like me, the majestic wilderness of this land is approaching a turning point. So too are the people. We and the natural world will keep on transforming in the ceaseless movement of all things. This illustrates, I believe, that the relationship between humanity and nature is an eternal theme with no resolution.

Still, all of us search in our lives for a better way to be. Some abandon comfort and convenience for the wilds. Others, like the Inuit and their fellow indigenous peoples, face manifold challenges as they rush into modernity. I want to observe firsthand the choices that people make through all these transitions. I want to know what sort of map the people I have met will draw in their lives. For their destinies are in some way bound to my own.

I seem to be rambling. Blame my revery on this worn-out diary, reappearing out of nowhere to put me in touch with a distant version of myself who I desperately long for. Fifteen years is supposed to be long, but doesn't it also feel surprisingly short?

I'm left wondering if I could ever go back to who I was then. To that forceful and frenzied inspiration that drove me to embark, compass lost, my trusty map gone blank. To a new voyage, port of arrival unknown. Perhaps such voyages are integral to all our lives in many ways.

Okay, it's about time I set down my writing brush.

A week from now, salmon will surge up the rivers. In the violent springing force of a salmon grasped in both hands, I always feel the Alaskan summer. Until next time.

June 1st, 1993

Red Bluff Cove

I'm on a journey through the Southeast Alaskan seas. Another day living aboard a boat is coming to a close. Although nothing of particular note happened, it was a full and satisfying day, so I decided to pick up my writing brush anyway, wanting to tell someone about it.

We've been chasing humpback whales for almost three weeks now. Hardly a short trip by any means, but at least we don't need to worry about running short on fresh food. The ocean here is so teeming with catch that you can pull in crab and salmon whenever you feel like it, with halibut three feet long. The water may not be the clearest, but that's just a sign of how rich it is – literally a soup of plankton.

Fall draws closer. The season of never-ending day has concluded with the return of night. I wouldn't be surprised if the northern lights appear. Believe it or not, I once saw them on these seas in midsummer. This would have been the month of July some four or five years ago. The midnight sun kept darkness at bay, and yet the glow of the aurora was so intense it bled through the brightness of the sky.

Throughout this journey, I've been thinking of a friend who I'll call O. Every time I encounter a new piece of scenery, I find myself wishing he were here. O has sunk into despair after losing his child in an accident and I want to show him this land-ringed sea, bordered on all sides by deep primeval forest.

This afternoon we came across a humpback whale with her calf. A rare mirror-like calm had fallen on the water, and we spotted faint blasts of their white breath in the distance. We approached slowly at first and then drove ahead to slip in beside them, coasting along with the engines turned low. The whales didn't seem to mind at all. On the contrary, they swam directly beneath our small boat again and again as though trying to play with us.

At one point the calf suddenly changed course. Breaking off from her mother, she gently closed in on the boat and looked up at us for a brief moment. That's all that happened really; we must have spent another two hours with them. By then the sun was beginning to tilt towards the horizon, time for us to find a sheltered place where we could dock for the night.

'Let's go to Red Bluff Cove.' This had been our plan since morning.

One of the marvels of Southeast Alaska is the beauty of its countless bays and inlets, each a microcosm of pristine nature devoid of any signs of humankind. The intricate fjord topography carves up a sea filled with islands in countless shapes and sizes, all coated in glaciers and virgin forest.

The most fun part about traveling here, perhaps, is getting to choose which little shoreline recess to anchor in.

If it's true that everyone has their own secret place of such magnificence that they want to keep it to themselves, for me that has to be Red Bluff Cove. I discovered it five years ago when taking refuge here during a storm. Red Bluff Cove is located on the eastern side of Baranof Island, with its stretches of mountains nestled around glaciers. True to the name we have chosen, the bluffs that form the entrance have a reddish tinge, which gives them a mysterious aspect under the fading light of dusk. From this narrow mouth, the cove gradually widens as you move inward, extending over a mile.

Of all the numerous inlets I have visited around here, I have found none as stunning and enigmatic. Never on any of my annual visits have I spotted another ship. In fact, no one I have ever met knows about this cove, though I've spoken to local fishermen with years of experience voyaging the whole region. I suppose the chances are slim that someone will venture into one little nook in these vast waters unless they have some kind of reason.

I remember one time I harbored here, this would have been three years ago, when I heard a strange call in the night. *Shwoosh, shwoosh* it went, arising from the silence and the darkness – the sound of a humpback whale that had strayed into Red Bluff Cove. I have many memories from this place. Every time I come here I sense the everlasting, a great current of time apart from our own that partakes of neither happiness nor sadness and helps us forget our daily striving, if only briefly.

It was around twilight that we entered the cove today, gazing up at its ocher cliffs. As we passed a swathe of shallow reefs and were putting more distance between us and the outer sea, we found ourselves slipping into a new world, as though turning the page of a book.

First was the silence. An all-subsuming silence. Evergreen leaves of spruce and hemlock spilled out to the shore; mist twined like a thing alive through primordial forest. Powerful wings sounded overhead as a bald eagle rose suddenly from the trees and wheeled off out of sight. The majestic bird had been watching us from the moment we arrived. Some thirty spotted seals congregated on a small island that had emerged with the ebb tide. And carefully observing the surface of the water on which our boat continued ahead, I could make out a seamless black band running on both sides. An enormous school of pink salmon come to spawn. Then, through gaps that opened up in the ancient trees cladding the mountainside, a waterfall poured down with incredible force. Looking upwards, it was only visible for some three hundred feet, above which it vanished into the woods, the source of its water a glacier on the peak.

The cove went on cutting long and narrow into the land, swelling and constricting like a lake as the mountains ahead loomed ever closer, untouched and untrodden. Eventually we reached the end and put down anchor.

Once the engine was off, true stillness enveloped us, and gradually we began to hear sounds that had previously escaped our notice. The cooing of birds, perhaps the chicks of a bald eagle, though looking around the woods there was no sign of them. The splash of a salmon that has leapt almost a foot into the air. The faint rushing of water from the direction of a valley, either a river or a waterfall.

As there was still some time until sunset, we lowered a rowboat stowed onboard and set out to explore, following a bank jutting with immense mossy trees. From the densely woven undergrowth bloomed nameless flowers of summer's end. There I spotted the red glitter of salmon berries, reached my hand overboard to pick some and put them straight in my mouth.

In its furthest reaches the cove turned to grassy plain, onto which the incoming tide was lapping. Cleanly trodden grass formed a road that led into the depths of a glen: the path of a bear visiting from the mountains to hunt salmon each day.

Intrigued by a brook flowing from a steep-sided ravine, we decided to go upstream as far as the boat would take us. In the murky water around fallen wood rested innumerable salmon. Glancing up, I saw a bald eagle perched in a huge hemlock, staring at us implacably. She seemed almost close enough to touch, and I wondered why she chose not to take flight.

Eventually the river grew too shallow to proceed and we decided to ride the current back to where we started. Already the sun had slipped behind the ridges and darkness was setting in around us. Apart from the sound of the wind passing through valleys, over glacier-hugging mountains and between moss-coated trees, perfect silence reigned. In this grand landscape, unaltered by others of our kind, we were the only things that moved. All I could think was how I wanted to bring my friend O here one day.

The night deepened and the sky filled with stars. We waited for the northern lights to no avail but were greeted by the moon instead.

I'm hoping to return again next year to my secret hideaway, Red Bluff Cove.

August 15th, 1993

Fall in Northern Lands

I'm currently walking through the September wilds of Alaska, in a section of the vast alpine tundra that spreads from the foot of Denali. The beauty of fall in northern lands is beyond compare.

This morning I heard a chorus of honking Canada geese. But looking up at the azure sky I could not see them anywhere. On a more careful search I made out a V formation approaching from the north. The flock was flying so high it had eluded me. This was their fall migration. Nesting in the Arctic Circle complete, the geese are on a journey back south.

From the prime vantage of the hill I stand upon, I see mountains of deepest north coated in a fine layer of fresh snow. A wind carrying the faint scent of winter eases my sweat-coated body. When I remove the backpack digging into my shoulders to take a brief rest, I spot perched in the vegetation of the tundra a small bird with a scarlet beak. I have never seen such a bird before and approach slowly, wondering what kind it could be, then realize that it is merely wearing the vivid red lipstick of lingonberries just pecked.

The brief Alaskan fall begins with the leaves of aspen and silver birch turning yellow and the carpet of the tundra taking on the hue of red wine. Day by day these colors deepen in the wilds until the manifold plants of the tundra form a mosaic inexpressibly sublime. Then it is all clear skies and sunshine until one chilly evening arrives and you wake up the next morning to find the scenery has shifted. In a single night the autumn has leaped ahead with the passage of the north wind's paintbrush. Much like the new green of spring, the peak lasts but a day.

Meanwhile, blueberries and lingonberries ripen. These are picked busily by bears and migratory birds, both of them storing up fat – one to hibernate over the long winter, the other to complete the long flight south. The bounty of nature in the north differs from that in southern climes, containing within it a certain frenetic tension, condensing and then instantly scattering in an extreme environment.

'How are the blueberries this year?' This becomes a seasonal Alaskan greeting as people take after the wildlife in storing up the abundance of fall for life in the winter.

I'm now growing tired from hiking this autumn mountain and decide that it's due time to stuff my mouth with blueberries. All you have to do is find some foliage through which bunches of blue fruit peek, plump yourself down on the ground, eat every berry within reach and then crawl a few yards away to start again. Soon I realize that I've stained my trousers red and blue yet again this year.

In this season we often tell those going to pick blueberries, 'Don't knock noses with a bear.' This is not entirely a joke. Both people and bears tend to move around in a blueberry-gobbling trance and forget where they are. It will sometimes occur to me that I'm not paying attention to my surroundings, whereupon I cautiously look around.

Such moments invariably call to mind *Blueberries for Sal*, a picture book about a mother and son who decide one fall to go blueberry-picking in the mountains. The boy Sal follows behind his mother while she is engrossed in collecting berries, then strays from her without either of them realizing. Meanwhile, a mother bear and her cub have come to the same mountain. When the cub similarly strays from his mother while she absorbedly devours berries, the boy ends up following the mother bear and the cub ends up following the mother human, unbeknown to any of them. The book is actually pretty realistic in the context of Alaska.

While crossing a swathe of mountain-valley scree, I hear an adorable chirping call. I stop to scan the area and find a pika sitting on the very top of a large boulder, its mouth full to bursting with hay. When the small rabbit-like animal bolts away, I track its path to a gap in the rocks into which it seems to have vanished. Crouching to peer in, I find a neatly piled bedding of hay. The critter has been stocking up in preparation for the long winter on its way.

I mount a rise and gaze into the distance, where I spot a herd of caribou trotting along the foot of a distant mountain.

They must be heading to southerly woodlands below the tree line for the winter. A fawn grown large since its birth in spring follows close after its mother. Their epic journey is at last approaching its end.

Near a lake at dusk I come across a moose mother with her calf – her only remaining calf. Cows usually give birth in pairs but it's rare to see the trio together by this time of year. Many moose are killed within a month of their birth by wolves and bears; one is usually lost as it is difficult for the mother to protect two young simultaneously.

Right now must be the peak of the luminous colors that dye the wilds before me. The day is not far off, after the daily geese formations overhead have vanished into the southern horizon and the aurora begins to dance in the clear night sky, when the autumn will have perceptibly paled. It can't be more than a week away.

Despite its incredible beauty, fall somehow sets our emotions into a flurry. Is this because the fleeting summer of the deep north has faded in a gasp? Or because the long dark winter will presently arrive? Yet all it takes to prepare us and restore calm to our hearts is the coming of first snowfall. I love these intimations of fall. In the revolution of one season to the next, we can sense the time that flows into the fathomless beyond. Wondrous are the workings of nature. How many times will the fleeting things we encounter each year come and go with the melancholy of their passing? Keep count of these meetings to grasp the brevity of a human life. This is what the Alaskan fall means to me.

September 5th, 1993

Tidings of Spring

How is everything where you are?

Here the signs of March in the air tell me that the worst of winter is over. That pummeling sixty-below cold will visit us in Fairbanks no more. The daylight hours are lengthening rapidly, and in my heart it already feels like spring. Of course not all regions of Alaska are experiencing these changes just yet. In northern latitudes sixty-seven degrees and above, where the Inuit and other indigenous peoples of the Arctic Circle reside, many days of harsh weather are still to come.

Snowfall was heavy this winter, and word is that hungry moose have been turning up near homes around town. They know about the vegetable gardens that many of us keep in the summer and come down from the mountains to eat any crops left unharvested beneath the snow. At thirteen to fifteen hundred pounds, these gigantic animals hardly resemble deer as many imagine and are an alarming sight when they emerge without warning from the woods in your yard. Moose can indeed be dangerous, especially mothers with their young, and care must be taken never to approach them. Still, when you spot a living being striving desperately to survive right next to your daily abode, it's hard not to stop what you're doing and watch them for a while. The sight braces you in a certain way for your own challenges.

As I write this, my wife Naoko is pregnant. I am at once overjoyed and anxious about this development. Naoko continues to have intermittent spotting and we're worried about the possibility of a miscarriage. After consulting with the local doctor, we have decided to wait and see how her condition progresses. Although I've been involved with the immense wilderness of Alaska for many years, this is my first time feeling perplexed by a little slice of nature of my own.

Some six or seven years ago, I caught my first sight of a caribou giving birth. This was while I was up north awaiting their spring migration. From my campsite the Arctic Ocean was visible on the edge of the horizon, and even though it was the month of May the wind made the air feel like minus fifty.

One day around twilight, a small herd of caribou descended from the mountains. There must have been thirty to forty of them in total. They had journeyed over six hundred miles, all the way from the woodlands of Arctic Canada. The entire herd was female, and I knew that most would be bearing young. While I had been following the caribou for close to a decade, I had yet to witness a birth. Since I could only ever stake out one spot at a time in the vast Alaskan Arctic through which the caribou are constantly on the move, my chances of encountering this momentous event were slim.

But as I watched through binoculars from my tent, one fell behind the rest of the herd, behaving strangely. In a panic, she kept tumbling to her side and getting back up again. I decided that she must be about to give birth. She was too far away to photograph and I would have startled her if I'd left the tent, so I stayed where I was, squeezing the binoculars in my fists with eager anticipation. Her companions, not breaking pace, had already vanished into the distance of the tundra.

When the lone caribou stood up suddenly, a small black form flopped out onto the snowy field. Hurriedly I stuffed a camera into my backpack and crawled as quietly as I could out of my tent, then made my way on all fours towards them until they were in close view. I believe it was around midnight, but the season of endless day was upon us and the sun that never sets shone on the white plane. Even bundled up as I was in thick down gear, the burning cold cut through to my skin.

The mother licked the new life from head to toe with fierce attention and eventually rose into position to give milk, whereupon the calf staggered over on rubbery legs and latched on to her teat. Depleted of energy, the mother presently began to eat her fallen placenta from the ground. When the midnight sun had slid along the horizon to turn seamlessly into the morning sun and then began to rise, the calf followed unsteadily after its mother; before I knew it both were out of sight.

It was a few days later that I found the carcass of a small calf frozen on the side of a river. Whether it had been killed by a wolf or a bear or had died of natural causes was unclear; in any case, half of it had already been eaten. The incidence of mortality for caribou young is concentrated in their first week, a period that divides those that survive from the rest. I couldn't tell whether the body was that of the newborn I had seen. But I remember even now my astonishment at how clear-cut these scenes of life and death were.

Something else happened to me recently. I was at home reading a book when I heard a thud on one of the windows. Hurrying out to the porch, I found a redpoll curled up below the pane of glass. The bird had slammed right into the surface, where the trees were reflected distinctly. The impact must have been quite hard; when I put her in the palm of my hand I found that her head was bleeding. As it was a chilly early-spring day, I decided to bring her indoors and placed her in a small paper box to watch over her for a while.

Nearly all birds in Alaska are migratory; only a scarce minority stick it out through Fairbanks' subpolar winter. Redpolls are one such variety, and I often wonder how a tiny bird only four inches in length can endure such inhospitable cold. This one was injured and had to breath with the entirety of her small frame. As much as I wanted to save her, I didn't know what I could do. At the same time, it was strangely moving to watch the lifeblood of this delicate being drain away.

A few hours later I put her back on the porch. I had no idea if she would recover on her own and fly away, or be attacked and eaten by another bird or perhaps a squirrel. When I checked outside in the evening, she was gone.

Both the birth of a caribou on a snowfield blasted by icy winds and the singing of a redpoll in the frigid Arctic air remind us of the inherent strength of life. Yet beneath such strength nature always conceals fragility – and it is this fragility that fascinates me more.

Our continued existence from one day to the next is in no way guaranteed; it may just be a miracle. Ultimately, the same is true of your heart pumping in your chest at this very moment. The same is also true of babies being born into this world. Amid my anxiety about the possibility of my wife miscarrying, I was becoming attuned to the tenuousness of life.

'When a woman's pregnancy is going to end early, there's nothing you can do to change it,' my mother-in-law had told us. 'It's something natural so just leave it to take its course.'

No words could have eased our minds more than this advice. We subsist inside the bounds of our inherent fragility; that is, human life is sustained only within certain limits. It's all too easy to forget this.

In another month the thaw will begin. At this time last year, the snow that had piled up on our roof froze into a single mass and slid off the edge one morning, smashing our porch. I was startled out of my wits by this tiding of spring.

The cold will return again and we will no doubt see snowfall many times more. But proceeding and retreating as it goes, a new season is assuredly on its way. Goodbye for now.

March 7th, 1994

Wolves

I've come alone to Ruth Glacier, one of several glaciers that
drape the southern slopes of Denali. This may very well be the
most breathtaking landscape in the entire Alaska Range. The
beauty comes as much from the glacier itself as the overawing
majesty of the rock pinnacles that spear upward around its
fluid icy form. The monolithic granite cliffs. The deep blue
of calved glacier cross-sections. The intricate contours of
immense crevasses. This barren landscape, where no flower
blooms, where no living thing is to be found, seems to refuse
any who would enter. And yet, it possesses a mysterious power
to cleanse and uplift the human heart.

These qualities are found nowhere more so than the area
at the head of the glacier where I set up basecamp every year,
Ruth Amphitheater.* This ancient natural amphitheater is

---

* Now commonly known as the Don Sheldon Amphitheater.

formed by an encirclement of mountains that rise to some three miles in height. Words offer no comparison for the lofty magnificence of the scenery. When I come here, I often recall the words of mythologist Joseph Campbell. He once wrote of 'a sacred place where the walls and laws of the temporal world may dissolve to reveal a wonder.' When asked about this idea in an interview, Campbell replied:

> This is an absolute necessity for anyone today. You must have a room, or a certain hour or so a day, where you don't know what was in the newspapers that morning, you don't know who your friends are, you don't know what you owe anybody, you don't know what anybody owes to you. This is a place where you can simply experience and bring forth what you are and what you might be. This is the place of creative incubation. At first you may find that nothing happens there. But if you have a sacred place and use it, something eventually will happen.

Later in the interview, Campbell continues: 'People claim the land by creating sacred sites, by mythologizing the animals and plants – they invest the land with spiritual powers.'

Last night was a full moon. When its lambent round face rose over the shoulder of a massive rock peak known as Moose's Tooth, the entire glacier glowed even as the encompassing mountains cast their shadows upon it. Unable to sit still on such a night, I put a thermos of coffee in my backpack and skied from the campsite crags to the glacier in one swift descent.

It may be March but these are high-alpine conditions. My body stung with the cold of the night wind blowing across the glacier. Still, there is nothing like the sound of skis carving through a world of total silence. And I felt more and more as though I belonged in this vast landscape.

I came to a stop before the white undulations of the snowfield that mark the beginning of the crevasses concealed deep beneath. These prevented me from proceeding to the dead center of Ruth Glacier but I was far enough out to feel as though I was already there. For Moose's Tooth, Mount Barrille, Mount Salisbury and Denali were on full display in a ring all around me.

I put down my backpack and, sipping hot coffee from my thermos, allowed myself to just be in the middle of a glacier lifted by moonlight from the night. Other than the occasional rumble of an avalanche somewhere, nothing stirred or made a sound. Shooting stars fell in rapid succession like rain through the dark glittering sky. The moment strikes me as something like the desert of a night my friend who traveled the Sahara once recounted to me, the uncanny energy that a realm of nothing but sand and stars endows to the human being.

Living in a world overflowing with information, we seem to have forgotten that any other kind of world even exists. So when flung by chance into somewhere like this, we find ourselves stalling in bewilderment. But if we remain still for a time, we begin to regain piece by piece the abundance that a place of scarce information brings, retrieving from oblivion a sort of strength or imaginative power that we have lost.

There was an odd incident at camp this afternoon: a snow bunting alighted right beside my tent. When I crept closer, it showed no signs of fear. It was odd to see the bird here in this alpine glacial region, lacking in anything it might have eaten. Certainly no environment for a small passerine to casually pause in. Perhaps it had gotten lost or was in the progress of migrating, but all such explanations felt implausible to me. When I tossed the bird some food, it showed no interest and just flitted around the tent as though trying to tell me something. Soon enough, I realized that the bunting was gone. It was a curious time that the bird and I shared in this lifeless place.

The encounter called to mind a fly that features in a Navajo myth I once read. When people walked through the desert, the fly would occasionally buzz over and perch on their shoulders. It was known as Little Storm and would whisper into the ear of a fledgling hero subjected to some trial the answers to difficult questions posed by their father. In other words, it was the voice of the sacred spirit disclosing secret wisdom.

I have one memory from Ruth Glacier that I have kept almost entirely to myself. It is from the first time I visited more than a decade ago.

I was skiing swiftly down from basecamp to the glacier just like last night, when I spotted a line of tracks on the snowdrifts piled atop the crevasse zone. The tracks stretched from the direction of Denali and continued endlessly down Ruth Glacier. Wondering what might have left the marks, I approached to discover that they were the paw prints of a wolf. I could not begin to fathom why there would be a wolf in this glacial region. Could the animal have taken a wrong turn like the snow bunting earlier today? Or did it travel here over the three-mile-high ridges of Denali? The episode just seemed too far-fetched and too conveniently like a good yarn for me to bring myself to tell anyone. Isn't it peculiar how memories shut up inside us retain an unaccountable power? Whenever my mind turns to Ruth Glacier during my daily routine in the city, as it does on occasion, the image of that one wolf's tracks invariably comes to me. There can be no doubt that a wolf once journeyed alone through this sterile landscape of rock and ice. If I pause to contemplate this, I can't help feeling that it is a very sacred place.

Almost one week has passed since I arrived at Ruth Glacier. My face is tanned a dark brown. The nights grow steadily shorter, and I sense with certainty the arrival of spring even in this elevated land of snow. The crash of avalanches comes more frequently today.

March 25th, 1994

From the Galapagos

I'm currently in Ecuador. Everything here is new and fascinating to me. The appearance of the indigenous peoples is so unlike what I'm accustomed to back home in Alaska. They make me feel like I've come to some strange and nameless land. It's as though I'm taking my first trip abroad all over again.

After a midnight takeoff from San Francisco, I woke up inside the cabin the following morning to find the landscape of South America already spread out below me. The subequatorial geography made for some odd and exotic vistas to someone coming from just below the Arctic. For here I was looking at an extreme high-altitude mountain region and yet I could see neither glacier nor snow. On the contrary, trees grew almost to the peaks. Now and then I would spot an isolated village in one of the valleys and find myself riveted until it slipped from view, utterly incapable of imagining what life there might be like, enthralled as ever by scenes of human habitation.

I was still struggling to accept that I had arrived so quickly at this distant continent. My body and emotions just couldn't keep up with the pace of travel. Truth be told, beneath the thrill of taking in the novel scenery beyond the window, I was even somewhat uneasy. It was the discomfort of grasping 'the world' through immediate sensations even though the word refers to an abstraction containing infinite expansiveness. This perception was reminiscent of the perplexing loneliness that comes over us when we perceive sweeping concepts like 'humankind' and 'planet Earth' as something finite. You may find these observations silly in this day and age, as the twenty-first century approaches, but they express honest impressions that I cannot entirely shake off.

I was reminded of a story that I had once read. It is about an archeological expedition to a dig site in what I seem to recall was the Andes Mountains. The survey team forms a large caravan and travels through the mountain ranges of South America with indigenous alpine guides hauling their luggage, until one day they stop and adamantly refuse to take another step. The desperate team offers to raise their daily wages if only the guides will immediately get going again, assuming the guides are staging a demand for better pay. But they keep their feet planted, unwilling to even hear their employers out. Finally, a member of the team who can speak the local language asks the guides' representative what on earth is the matter, to which the representative is said to have replied:

'We walked too quickly and have left our minds behind. We shall wait here until our minds catch up.'

I am here in Ecuador as part of a photobook initiative involving some thirty photographers gathered from across the globe. Each of us has been assigned to a different locale, which we will spend two weeks shooting. During this brief period, we are to focus our energies on some particular theme, ranging from the Amazon region to the indigenous peoples, to tropical rainforests, and the resulting images will be collected in a single publication. Although the project is sponsored by the government of Ecuador, editors from *National Geographic* (USA), *GEO* (France) and *Airone* (Italy) will jointly handle the task of compilation. Proceeds from the photobook's sale will then go to supporting Ecuadorian photographers.

I have been put in charge of the Galapagos. Since regulations ban staying overnight on any of the islands in the chain, I am living on a boat and traveling from island to island. Not long ago, a wildfire on Isabela Island made headlines around the world, raising fears that the habitat of the rare Galapagos tortoise might have been destroyed, but the fire was completely extinguished by the time I arrived.

Ten days since departing Alaska for this trip, I still feel like I'm in another universe. From the world's largest tortoise, the equatorial penguin, and the flightless cormorant whose wings degenerated due to an abundance of food to be had by diving into the sea, to iguanas who remind us of geological history and finches who evolved on each of the islands into a total of thirteen* different species, all the organisms here are strange and unreal. When I gaze at the marvelous sunsets over the South Sea, I can't help imagining the HMS *Beagle* appearing over the ocean horizon some one hundred and fifty years ago.

The funny thing is that even as I relish the unique natural environment of the Galapagos Islands I find myself yearning for Alaska. At this time of year, great caribou herds are crossing the Arctic tundra. Could they have already passed through the Kongakut River valley where I always make camp? If the mosquitoes are numerous this year, I bet those beasts are bunched together in a massive drove. My bush-pilot friend Don Ross could be flying over the Brooks Range at this very moment. I'm helplessly preoccupied with such ruminations. As enthralling as my first time abroad is proving to be, the pull of Alaska on my emotions only grows stronger by the day.

The most gratifying part of participating in this Ecuadorian project has been the opportunity to meet several South American photographers. In particular, I have really hit it off with Colombian cameraman Aldo Brando, who has been assigned to the Galapagos alongside me; after traveling together these past days, he now feels almost like a brother.

Aldo's consistent photographic subject has been Colombia's natural environment. The Amazon portion of the country is an inexhaustible source of inspiration for him. Hearing him talk about it gives me a visceral rather than merely factual

---

* Now thought to number eighteen.

grasp of the rapid change that its ecologies and ways of life are undergoing. Every night he speaks passionately to me of his goal as a photographer: to leave a record of a world in the process of vanishing.

At the same time, he confides in me about the trials and tribulations of making a living from photography in Colombia. Forget a dedicated nature magazine; his country lacks any kind of media that publish photos. The more I listen, the more clearly his life of poverty crystallizes for me. He has no proper home, nor any belongings to speak of aside from his photographic gear – and even this is not entirely up to scratch. It is hard to believe that this is the state of the nature photographer representing Colombia on this project.

Even so, Aldo is decisive, has a philosophical streak, and can be funny in a way I don't know how to describe. The little speech he gave when everyone was introducing themselves before we set off has stuck with me.

'I take photographs of Colombia's natural environment. It makes me kind of sad to think that when you all hear the word Colombia, you're picturing the mecca of crime and narcotics . . .Our nation doesn't have the luxury to put effort into wildlife conservation, but I hope to protect the ways of life and ecologies of the Amazon as best I can by continuing to capture it . . .Oh, and I also rock climb. I like to scale sheer cliffs over the sea. It's hard to explain but this is more a kind of faith for me than a hobby. Nice to meet you all.'

There's something otherworldly about Aldo. And I am drawn to his simple and devoted humanity. Before participating in this project, Colombia – or I should say South

America as a whole? – was hard for me to put my finger on. Now it feels almost familiar. This is thanks to the story of Aldo, my newfound friend. The more you grow to love a person that you meet, the more depth and breadth the landscape carries. Ultimately, I'd like to believe that the world implies an infinite expanse.

On that note, watching the sunset on the equator really threw me for a loop. In Alaska, the sun slides with almost perfect horizontal slowness to the horizon, whereas here it plummets straight towards the ocean, turning the world to night in an instant.

June 28th, 1994

Old Crow

How is everything over there? With July soon to arrive, the weather here remains hot. Contrary to popular belief that Alaska is always cold, Arctic summer is dry and invigorating, hardly raising a sweat.

I have arrived at a Gwich'in village called Old Crow. Located just barely across the national border with Canada, it stands on the bank of the Porcupine, a beautiful river of the deep north that runs from Arctic Canada to Alaska, where it empties into the great Yukon.

In keeping with the name Old Crow, I see many ravens as I walk through the village. But they fly off at the slightest suggestion you will approach, as though discerning human intentions. The raven is a fixture in the creation myths of many Alaska Natives, depicted as a mysterious being endowed with a kind of strange power. In these tellings, Raven created the world. They say he made it a happy place at first, free of ugliness and suffering, then grew tired of the world's perfection and crafted it again as something incomplete. And so human beings were born as one of Raven's many flawed creations. All stories aside, isn't it a great name for a town?

The Gwich'in are congregating in Old Crow this year as part of a biannual festival. Although I flew in by Cessna, most of the visitors seem to have traveled here by boat along the river. They come from communities like Arctic Village, Chalkyitsik and Venetie, that appear on a map to be separated from Old Crow by the border but that you can tell from the air all reside in the same wilderness. However you find your way to this place, there is no sense at any point of crossing a dividing line.

Have you ever heard of the Gwich'in tribe? I doubt many Americans have either. Numbering less than five thousand in total, the Gwich'in are a hunting people who depend upon the waves of caribou that roll through the land. If not for a dispute over the future of the Arctic that embroiled the USA, concerning a choice between oilfield development and protecting the environment that sustains the caribou, and if not for the Gwich'in raising their voices in protest, they might have remained forgotten in their remote corner of the Arctic to this day. This is no doubt what they would have preferred.

The influx of festival participants from the various towns swells Old Crow's population of little more than two hundred to twice that number. Since the homes of the villagers cannot accommodate them all, most set up tents along the riverside – myself included. On the introduction of an indigenous friend,

I am supposed to stay in the tent of a woman named Lorrie, who I have never met.

I have come out here with only the vague instruction to look for a big green tent, but thankfully I manage to find it right away. Lorrie looks to be in her mid-thirties. She has two children and, like her parents – a Gwich'in mother and white father – she is already divorced. Her brooding expression makes me somewhat concerned for her. She has come all this way hauling a tent by herself. When I ask her nonchalantly why she is joining the assembly, her only reply is, 'For personal reasons.'

While this Gwich'in congregation held every two years is called a festival, it primarily serves as a communal site for everyone to air the various issues they face. Each day a topic is decided and then discussed from morning to night. Worries about oilfield development, protecting the hunting way of life, loss of traditional values, alcoholism, the fading of their language, the future of the young . . . A litany of problems confronted not only by the Gwich'in but by Alaska Natives at large as they teeter on the edge of a new era.

Anyone who has something to say can step up to the mic in whatever order and speak for as long as they like. Some relate memories, others offer confessions, fears, dreams for the future. The only rule is that speakers must hold a wooden staff prepared for the occasion. In these customs, I sense the firm intention to unify the wishes of all. Now and then I search for Lorrie among the crowd.

I myself don't have a clear practical objective in coming to Old Crow, except that, through photographing caribou for nearly a decade, I have developed a fascination with the hunting peoples of the deep north, who have subsisted in step with these wanderers, and am gradually beginning my own journey to better understand them. My hope is to speak with Gwich'in elders and ask them how people used to think, what sort of relationship they had with nature. But I'm not just angling to hear tales of yore; I want to meet as many people as opportunity presents and try to understand the circumstances of their lives.

As I sit in a corner of the assembly space listening to the speakers, I am surprised to discover that the problems of the Gwich'in abiding in the Arctic wilds are at once our problems as well. They can all be summed up in a single phrase: anxiety about the new era. This feeling is directed both outward to the natural environment that surrounds the Gwich'in and inward to their own minds. I hear many complain that they no longer know what to believe as values diversify on the verge of modernization. It makes me wonder what course I would chart if I were a Gwich'in youth. I can't help being moved by the sight of people desperately seeking a better way forward in a predicament from which all exits seem blocked.

We live in a truly dumbfounding time, only five years from the second millennium. Resource depletion, overpopulation, pollution . . . Just thinking about it for a moment is enough to paralyze you. Perhaps we need to find the right answer. But here's what I believe: that there was never going to be a right answer to begin with. Adopting this perspective can be a real load off your shoulders. It's a relief to know that we're not required to be correct.

Being told that we must be responsible for humankind and for the Earth a thousand years into the future is overwhelming. Pretty words do not a realistic plan for the distant future make. But here's what I also believe: even if a thousand years is impossible, we're responsible for the world one, maybe two hundred years from now. In other words, even though we lack the right answer, we have a duty to steer ourselves in a better direction within our own era. Which is to say, both we and the Gwich'in will always be on a journey.

As the gathering winds to a close on the final day, Lorrie steps up to the mic.

'I've always lived in white people's society. With my parents' divorce and then my own, I lost sight of who I was, and pretty soon I started to think about the indigenous blood that makes up half of what flows through my veins. Looking back, I went through a really unstable childhood. I never understood what it was about.'

Lorrie speaks as though finally letting it all out.

'Then one time I visited the village where my mother was born and raised, and I sensed right away that that was where I belonged. Ever since, I've slowly begun to take part in Gwich'in gatherings.'

Afterwards, in the tent, I hear her mutter to herself, 'So glad I came to this gathering . . .' We are merely passing each other by in the village of Old Crow and know nothing of each other's lives. Still, I think to myself that she too is on a journey.

The Gwich'in gathering ends today. Last night, various foods revolving around the caribou were served, and the participants danced late into the night while filling their bellies with this land's natural bounty. They even managed to drag me into the circle.

It is another day of heat and sun. The Alaskan villagers will boat their way back down Porcupine River. Majestic wilds stretch without end. White watercolor clouds wisp the boundless sky. Into that blue a croaking raven fades.

July 4th, 1994

From Salzburg

I'm writing you this letter from Salzburg. It's my first time in Europe. Although the continent is just a short hop from Alaska by polar routes and I've been in the US for eighteen years, I just never got around to making the journey. Now that I'm here in Austria, I'm all elated like a child taking a field trip alone, or a country boy at last exploring Tokyo.

I initially flew to Düsseldorf to give a talk on the peoples and environment of Alaska at a film festival organized by the German Society for Nature Photography. I spent several days there until my part in the festival concluded, after which I found myself with a bit of time left over to travel by myself. But rather than rush about this way and that during my ten-day itinerary, I wanted to take it slow in a single destination. So I decided to spend the remainder of my brief sojourn in Salzburg, a city that has held an exalted place in my mind for many years and is home to an Austrian friend of mine.

When I mentioned *The Sound of Music* to him, he responded wearily, 'Not you too,' as if I were just like all the other tourists. But I couldn't help making the association; the scenery of Salzburg as captured in the film was one of my formative childhood memories. In those days, any country outside Japan seemed immeasurably far away, and I can still recall my puerile astonishment that the world could contain anywhere so beautiful, with that distinctive old city like something out of a storybook surrounded by the slopes and ridges of the Alps.

I departed Düsseldorf by morning train, gazing upon the Rhine and crossing mountain valleys before arriving late at night in Salzburg. My friend came to pick me up. As he drove me along the Salzach River that flows through the city, the medieval Hohensalzburg Fortress emerged from the nightscape and, coming as I had from the wilds of Alaska, I felt like I was in another universe. How wonderful it must be to live in a city where history exists not as knowledge but as a distinct presence within your surroundings. Such immediate connection to the past must alter the way that residents think, helping them to unconsciously grasp the invisible flow of time that gestures obliquely to their origin.

Rather than visit tourist attractions when I travel, I prefer to go to local cafés and outlying eateries to observe the expressions of the people, which is precisely how I'm wiling away the days in Salzburg when not strolling around. Each afternoon, I stop by Café Mozart to watch the patrons read newspapers or play chess as I sip my coffee. There's something curious about sitting just a few yards from a person whose life you know nothing about and with whom you will never be acquainted. These are the kinds of thoughts, as trivial as they may be, that occupy me when I travel in an unfamiliar land.

That reminds me. I went to a barber's shop today because my hair was growing long and here's my pet theory about it: if you're traveling somewhere and you want to get a sense of the people who live there, nothing beats going to a barber shop. I cannot explain exactly why, but when you sit in the barber's chair alongside the locals and let your mind wander while someone cuts your hair and shaves your beard, you begin to feel inexplicably as if you are from that place.

A Swiss person I met in Alaska once told me: 'Switzerland doesn't have any nature left. Nearly every inch of the land is managed and artificial. If there was some way to move mountains, we Swiss would have fine-tuned their positions by now.'

I finally understand on this trip why Alaska sees so many Swiss and German tourists. The reason became palpably clear to me a few days ago when I was climbing a mountain on the outskirts of Salzburg with my friend. The Alps looked to me then like a little toy garden compared to the sights I'm used to. They were very beautiful but without depth, the kind of natural environment that comforts, lacking in the majesty that seems to forbid human trespass. What draws Europeans to Alaska is the search for untamed bona fide wilderness.

A person who journeyed around Alaska over a century ago is reported to have said, 'You should never go to Alaska as a young man because you'll never be satisfied with any other place as long as you live.' The point is that visiting too early risks making everywhere else seem minuscule and insufficient by contrast. I don't believe for a second that large environments are superior to small ones. I'm just passing on the words of a traveler from olden times that I happened to recall.

What has amazed me most on this visit to Salzburg is the great antiquity of the architecture. The stone hall where I saw a classical concert last night has to be over three hundred years old. Hohensalzburg Fortress, visible wherever you go in the city, dates back to 1077. The shock of learning this has upended my perception of history and of time. I am surprised to find such artifacts of the distant past alive within modernity, even as I am forced to recognize anew that Roman civilization, the Renaissance and other elements of the Western story are much more recent than we tend to acknowledge.

In my travels across Alaska, I have come up with my own scale for measuring human history. It employs as its reference point Beringia, the land bridge that existed during the last Ice Age when the Bering Sea dried up, allowing ancient east Asian people to cross from northern Asia to North America some ten thousand years ago. As I grew used to thinking in terms of a ten-thousand-year duration, the Ice Age stopped seeming all that long ago. On the contrary, if you count backwards into the past using the span of a human life, it feels like just the other day.

In this light, European historical events seem so near to me. Standing in front of, say, a building from the Renaissance, I find myself astounded that this period was a mere four or five centuries back. Am I reacting to the shallowness of human history or to the speed at which our ways of life transform?

The best part about my first trip to the old continent is the opportunity to simultaneously hold the flow of time of two worlds, Europe and Alaska. It's an example of how experiencing something for yourself is completely different from hearing or reading about it in a book. Once I'm back home, I expect to renew my travels through Alaska with a fresh outlook.

Tomorrow I will go with my friend to a village in a mountain valley some thirty miles from Salzburg. He's taking me to his birthplace to meet his elderly parents. I'm told it's a beautiful village. I also hear that the nearby Hallstatt valley is home to the descendants of prehistoric rock-salt miners. I'm excited to visit.

Today there was a slight sprinkle of snow. I miss the Alaskan winter. Until next time.

October 28th, 1994

The Amish People

I'm currently visiting Pittsburgh, in the state of Pennsylvania. It's November, but coming from Alaska I can hardly feel a chill in the air. I relish the bracing cold of winter back home, even when it drops fifty below zero.

I've flown here to attend the opening ceremony for a photo exhibition titled 'Alaska', now on at the Carnegie Museum of Natural History and set to run for some three months. Traveling to big cities in mainland USA always makes me keenly aware of how far-flung my adopted home is. The place of my ever-so-normal daily routine begins to feel like a distant world apart.

Having nothing on the agenda today, I was brainstorming places to visit when I suddenly thought of the Amish, as Pennsylvania is home to several Amish villages. After doing a bit of research, I discovered that the closest was New Wilmington and decided to take a drive there.

The origin of the Amish dates to the Reformation in the beginning of the sixteenth century. They were a movement seeking a return to the frugal life of faith described in the Bible. This religious outlook has since been passed down generation to generation, with present-day adherents now living together in settlements made up exclusively of the like-minded. Extremely suspicious of technology, the Amish persist in eschewing the use of electricity, remaining aloof from modern civilization. Most forego a high-school education, few find employment outside their traditional communities and every family has a farm on which they eke out a simple life.

You have more than likely seen their distinctive dress in American movies. Men and boys alike wear wide-brimmed black hats and plain black clothes with no ornamentation of any kind. Females likewise wear unusual attire of unparalleled austerity. Horse-drawn box carriages are another symbol of the Amish. In a society designed around the automobile, nothing makes them stand out more. The presence of these contrarians in social form against the course of human history – these thoroughgoing skeptics of progress within a nation like the USA that gathers the cream of modernity – has long struck me as peculiar.

After a drive of some three hours, I arrive at New Wilmington, a typical rural American town but with an Amish village stretching along its periphery. I've heard that Amish communities are universally unwelcoming to outsiders – perhaps understandably, because, like me, many come as tourists just to get a look at them.

Passing through the town, I drive down a long sloping road into a beautiful stretch of countryside, when a black horse carriage suddenly appears right in front of the car. Or that is how it seems, given how much faster I'm going. Unsure at first how to manage the situation, I tail the carriage for a short while, then pass it at a low speed. In my rearview mirror, I glimpse the face of a man in the carriage. What stands out for me isn't the Santa Claus beard, nor is it the odd Amish outfit I am seeing for the first time. It is – how can I put this? – the impression his eyes give that he is thinking something entirely different from the rest of us. The black carriage grows ever smaller in the back mirror until finally it slips from view.

After a while I spot a small brick house on the edge of some farmland. It is an old seemingly neglected building only large enough for a single room. As I pass by, the door opens and Amish children in their traditional garb spring out. I have found the village school and feel now as though I've been transported two or three centuries into the past.

Driving through more picturesque countryside, I see other houses. None have cars parked out front, only those small black carriages. No power lines either. Wondering what their lives are like, I am overcome by the urge to take a peek inside.

'Quilts for sale', reads a sign in front of one house, and I decide to pull over. A little room at the back carries assorted village handicrafts. Stepping inside, I find a lovely twelve- or thirteen-year-old girl tending to the wares alone. Much as with my sighting of the Amish man riding the carriage, she makes a distinct impression on me. Again, it isn't her outmoded attire so much as the air she exudes, patently unlike that of a child brought up in the modern world. While I'm perusing the quilts, I glance up toward her to find that she has likewise been covertly watching me.

'Is there somewhere to eat in this village?' I ask, stupidly. Desperately wanting to exchange words, it is the best I can come up with. This Amish village obviously isn't going to have a restaurant.

An awkward pause follows before she replies.

'We don't have anywhere like that in this village, but there is a small shop on the edge of town where you can eat sandwiches...'

She speaks as if deeply ashamed. It occurs to me that she and her family may now and then travel into town by horse and carriage and have sandwiches at that shop. When an image of this outing pops into my head, it makes me both relieved and glad. I thank her, buy a small souvenir and leave.

I spend only a single day in the Amish village, one brief rove along that stretch of farmland. But each vista remains printed indelibly in my memory.

The young boy sitting all alone on a swing amid farmland hazed with smoke rising from the houses, as the sun began to sink. How did he spend the evening thereafter?

The pair of young men chatting, hoes in hands before a shed. What could they have been talking about?

The silhouette in the pale twilight of an elderly husband and wife driving horses to plow the land, like something out of a medieval landscape painting.

The history of human progress that we believed in, never doubted. Now we stand in a daze as the shadow inherent to that progress at last comes into view. But I'm left uncertain what significance the Amish might have to this predicament.

After eating at the shop the girl told me about, I stroll around the town of New Wilmington. Here the townspeople who reside in modernity and the Amish who turn their backs on it live side by side. What is it that divides these two worlds connected by one road? What sort of thing must that girl pass through when visiting the town by carriage and then pass through again when returning to the village? This indeterminate relationship seems to me beyond believing.

I wouldn't be surprised if that girl wishes in some part of her for town living awash in material things. Actually, I can't help hoping that she does. And there must be something that the people of New Wilmington for their part can't help thinking when they see the Amish girl in town.

Sun fully set, the warm lights of the main street turn on. With Thanksgiving approaching, a festive mood prevails in this small American town.

Suddenly I hear the clopping of a horse. Turning around, I watch a black carriage trundle over from across the street and blow past me. The carriage holds me transfixed. Even after I watch it disappear from sight, the sound of the horse's hooves stays with me, seeming to resonate perpetually in my body.

November 22nd, 1994

PART TWO

PART TWO

On Naoyuki Sakamoto

At Denali National Park this fall, I bumped into Dr Syoziro Asahina and his wife. I was standing by the side of the road watching a grizzly bear mother and cub on a distant slope, when the bus for Camp Denali lodge stopped in front of me and the old couple emerged bursting with excitement.

I had thought they might be arriving in Alaska soon but I wasn't expecting to come across them out here. In fact, I'd been worried that the trip would be too much for them, as the doctor's wife had been in poor health for some time and both were getting on in years. So I was elated to see their faces aglow with the thrill of faraway adventure, and before I knew it we were squeezing each other's hands.

Dr Asahina was retired from the University of Hokkaido, where he had been employed as a biologist with a specialization in insects from cold climates and had jointly led the Academic Alpine Club of Hokkaido during its formative years. The two of us had become acquainted three years earlier thanks to a series of serendipitous events involving the late painter Naoyuki Sakamoto, who I never had the honor of meeting.

It was February during the Sapporo Snow Festival. Scheduled to hold a photo exhibition in Sapporo for the first time, I had written an article for the local newspaper titled 'Thoughts on the Occasion of My Photo Exhibition'. When planning the article, I had decided on sudden inspiration to write about Naoyuki Sakamoto, whose paintings and essays had helped to nurture my passion for northern wilderness and the romantic notions of Hokkaido I had held since adolescence.

Born in 1906 in the city of Kushiro on the southeastern shore of Hokkaido, Naoyuki graduated from the Hokkaido University School of Agriculture before dedicating himself to pioneering the wilds of Tokachi, nearly forty miles southwest of his hometown. He proceeded to grapple for three decades with the barren land – a battle that he ultimately lost, at which point he traded his hoe for a paintbrush and became a landscape painter. His main subject was mountains, especially those in the Hidaka range that stretches to the south of Tokachi, but he also depicted the plains and fields across each phase of the four seasons.

Even more than his intrepid spirit, Naoyuki's paintings and the way they gestured to a life that had faced the land square on captivated me. Many of his essay collections, such as *Chronicle of Cultivation*, *View of Mountains from the Fields* and *Footprints in Snowfields*, still grace my bookshelf at home.

The world he conjured synergized with my yearning for the natural landscapes of Hokkaido and may have played some part in my taking an interest in Alaska.

When my photo exhibition opened, I was surprised to find among the visitors many of Naoyuki's mountaineering friends who had read my brief newspaper article. One of these was Dr Asahina. He had been Naoyuki's junior within the Academic Alpine Club while his wife was the painter's younger sister. It was due to our meeting then that the couple was now visiting Alaska.

Another of Naoyuki's friends present at the exhibition was a woman in her fifties. The two of us hit it off and soon found ourselves discussing *Footprints in Snowfields*. I told her that I was particularly fond of the first chapter, 'Song of Poroshiri'. Taking place in the late 1950s, it is an account of some old mountaineering friends who, weary of life, reunite for an expedition to the Hidaka range, including secluded Mount Poroshiri. Naoyuki's narration is heartwarming, allowing the reader to partake of the joy of the journey.

'This tranquil hidden place was once frequented by our predecessors the Ainu, who came to hunt bears,' he writes upon encountering the exquisite landscape of the enormous Nanatsunuma Cirque, nestled in the folds of Mount Poroshiri's hills, with its lingering snow and fields of flowers. 'For me it appeared to conceal legends and strange dreams.'

There was always something so compelling about Naoyuki's simple ruminations on the indigenous people of Hokkaido. Call it the perspective of a sorrow that is rooted in daily life and yet refuses to descend into nostalgia.

'I was with him for that climb to Poroshiri,' the woman told me proudly.

'You aren't perhaps the "young woman Ms I in charge of cooking who was right then in the market for a husband", are you?'

I could recall quotes like this almost word for word, having read the book numerous times. Although I had only just met this woman – who I'll refer to as Ms I, following *Footprints in Snowfields* – I began to feel close to her as though we had known each other for years.

During the period of my youth in which I discovered Naoyuki's work, I was drawn to the natural world of the north with a level of passion that amazes me when I think back on it. I was also an avid reader, for example, of a Hokkaido mountaineering magazine called *Northern Mountain Ranges* that was so obscure it could only be acquired at Meikeido bookstore in Tokyo. This despite the fact that I had yet to visit the island. Now here I was in Hokkaido's capital, meeting people from the stories that had so enchanted me.

To my disbelief, one day as the exhibition was winding down, Naoyuki's widow Tsuru showed up. In her late seventies, she presented herself with a tidy elegance, but an intimation of the living soil from their three-decade battle with the land still clung to her.

My most cherished memory connected to the exhibition was visiting Tsuru's home in the Teine area on her invitation and being treated to a lovingly prepared breakfast, one of the best I've had in my life. Butterbur-shoot suimono, warm rice . . . I couldn't stop asking for seconds and thirds.

When we were finished, I perused some old documents in the house and realized that Naoyuki was a descendant of one of modern Japan's founding fathers, Ryoma Sakamoto.

On my request, Tsuru showed me the collection of photos spread across several albums that recorded their harsh time as pioneers. It was both moving and amusing to note that the title of the series of albums had changed somewhere along the way from *Chronicle of Cultivation* to *Chronicle of Regret*, in a pun on the words for cultivation (開墾) and regret (悔恨), both pronounced *kaikon*. To struggle for three decades only to give up and leave it all behind . . . This was something that I couldn't fully comprehend as an adolescent. But Naoyuki affirmed the value of those years by taking up the paintbrush and now I understood that in the end he won. In light of all the time they spent in attaining this victory, the photo on the first page of Tsuru as an adorable young woman – barely more than a girl – has always stuck with me.

The most memorable section for me of *Footprints in Snowfields*, a book that I adore, is the story of an Ainu elder named Matakichi Hiro. Matakichi was said to have been innately attuned to nature from childhood. Even as Naoyuki was taken up with his efforts to cultivate the land, he would hike alone through the mountains of the southern Hidaka range, through which old man Matakichi also roamed in search of bears to kill. Since there were few pioneers of Naoyuki's sort in those days and the surrounding community was small, it was only a matter of time before word of his name reached

Matakichi. The scene of their meeting at the village blacksmith is beyond touching.

'This good for nothing here is Sakamoto,' the blacksmith says by way of introduction. 'Just like you, he goes romping about the mountains uninvited. I suppose you two louts are cut from the same cloth. But he's more liable to be scared out of his trousers at sight of a bear than to plug one.'

'Ah, Shakamoto,' Matakichi says in a peculiar drawl. 'I heard tell o' you. Wanted to mee'cha but you were'sn't around. Learned o' you when a fella said there's a general marching around these here mountains. What say you to that, General Shakamoto?'

'Is that what you heard? Well, I was hoping to meet you too, Matakichi. I'm delighted we've finally had the chance.'

After long ago being tricked and extorted out of the land he'd been given by the government, Matakichi lived in dire poverty through to old age. It was the unembittered and uncovetous attitude and charming personality that Matakichi retained despite these tribulations that gradually endeared him to Naoyuki.

One unforgettable incident that took place many years after their initial meeting is the night old man Matakichi shows up at Naoyuki's house in the wilds, his trusty antique Murata rifle slung over one shoulder. Face red and mood lightened from imbibing *shochu*, Matakichi regales them with bear-hunting tales and sings heart-piercingly plaintive Ainu lullabies, both of which deeply move Naoyuki, while to Naoyuki's children Matakichi seems like some messenger straight out of the world of fairy tales.

'What would you do, sir, if a bear came at you?'

'Well, I wouldn't slug 'er if I thought I'd miss the mark. When your old man here is lying in wait, they come my way. Sucker gets right near me not even realizing, got 'er head down – you can't slug 'er like that. Times like this I clear my throat real loud. That puts the shock into 'er and she stand up tall, all roaring like. Then she's just where I want 'er.'

The children gather in a circle around the old man, breath held, eyes wide, listening rapt to every astounding word that leaves his lips.

One day, when a ranger on patrol stops by Naoyuki's house, the conversation turns to old man Matakichi's age.

'According to his family register, Matakichi is eighty-six years old, born in January 1871, date unknown,' Sakamoto says, 'but the truth is that there are many years unaccounted for. Matakichi himself cites some two decades he's not sure about.'

'How could that be?' the ranger asks.

'It's just that Matakichi's year of birth doesn't add up with the things he says. For example, Matakichi claims he was the chief of his tribe back when the Tokachi Ainu and the Hidaka Ainu fought a war out behind this river a long time ago, though I couldn't tell you the decade. Young, sure, but he couldn't have been made chief as a ten- or even fifteen-year-old boy. He had to have been at least in his twenties . . . Word is Matakachi's the only person alive who still remembers where that battle happened.'

Later, Naoyuki takes the Sapporo-based poet and Ainu researcher Genzo Sarashina to visit old man Matakichi and establish his age despite the lacuna. The definitive evidence is taken from a story Matakichi tells about once visiting Sapporo. There he claims to have seen Ainu who had been forced to move to Hokkaido from Sakhalin Island and describes how their bearing was completely different from that of his own tribe. It turns out that this project of Ainu relocation occurred when Japan and Russia exchanged control of the Kuril Islands and a portion of Sakhalin as part of the Treaty of Saint Petersburg signed in 1875. According to the records, Matakichi would have been born four years earlier, but from the details of the story it was clear that he was at least approaching adolescence. In other words, old man Matakichi was roving around hunting bears with a gun, surviving off only the most meagre provisions and sleeping in the mountains, at the age of around one hundred.

At night on Christmas the year Matakichi learned this, he died.

Watched over by a small group of mourners, the sled bearing his coffin was pulled by hand to a cemetery on the plains within sight of the Pacific Ocean. I watched until the pitifully attended burial procession had traveled to the horizon of the snowy field and disappeared from sight . . . His empty house, devoid even of tools, looked profoundly lonesome after the loss of its owner. Over the bare earth floor, old man Matakichi's beloved rattletrap Murata rifle hung unceremoniously on a nail. Seeing this brought tears to my eyes as sadness welled up in me at last, and I rode my horse out into the snowy plain . . .

Upstream of the Nupuka Petsu river that the old man often waded through in life, the peak of Mount Omusha shone against the light of the evening sky. It was the star of nupuka (the plains) fallen to Earth.

By the time I read this passage as a teenager, the world it portrayed was already a thing of the past. Still, I dreamed of the northern wilds I had never seen and expected that I would one day live there. Yet in the end, I came to Alaska rather than Hokkaido. And a thought occurs to me as I write this. Perhaps in Alaska now, I am living out the era in Hokkaido that Naoyuki experienced and saw off with a kind of sorrow. Because while traveling through this land, I feel as though I have met many Matakichi Hiros. Inuit and Athabascan Matakichi Hiros.

The year after my exhibition in Sapporo, a letter arrived from Hokkaido. It was an invitation to the opening ceremony for the Naoyuki Sakamoto Memorial Hall that had been built on the outskirts of Obihiro. Naoyuki and I had never met. I was nothing more than a fan. Nevertheless, Tsuru had been kind enough to think of me.

The memorial hall was set to gradually exhibit Naoyuki's paintings from more than two decades of his wilderness residence in tandem with the seasons they represented. It had been built by Rokkatei, a long-established Hokkaido confectionary shop that supported Naoyuki's largely thankless work, using his paintings to create the beautiful distinctive flower design for some of its wrapping and as the cover image for the children's literary magazine *Sairo* that it continues to publish.

Although I was grateful for Tsuru's thoughtfulness, I couldn't make it out of Alaska just then. It wasn't until February of last year that I was finally able to visit. There could have been no more fitting site to commemorate Naoyuki Sakamoto. The memorial building was surrounded by a copse of oak trees, melding seamlessly with the surrounding landscape and evoking the land as it was in the pioneering age. As I crunched through the snow, I looked around at those oaks, still bearing dead leaves, and felt as though I had run into a long-lost acquaintance, for Naoyuki had often written of them. Ubiquitous to the terrain known as the wilds in Hokkaido, oaks are bemoaned by farmers as proof that the land is bad.

The first time I experienced winter in the plains, I saw the oak trees with their dead leaves still clinging even though snow had already piled up and took a strong interest in them. They were the ideal visual embellishment to the monotonous and bleak landscape, contributing the only warm hues to the otherwise exclusively cold color palette. The coarse and rugged oak is also incredibly supple and strong, serving a crucial role in supporting human life out here. Oak of the wilds, oaks and pioneers. There is no tree with which a cultivator of the land forms a deeper bond and hardly any tree that the mountain climber hiking these untamed flatlands retains more distinctly.

Visitors to the memorial hall were scarce in the off season, and quiet reigned over the grounds. The space of the interior was exceedingly welcoming, filled as it was with winter sunlight. I was delighted to see Naoyuki's work displayed in such an open and capacious setting. The floorboards creaked pleasantly under my feet as I circuited the exhibit, absorbing myself in each of his paintings. Some of the titles I recalled seeing in his books: *The Nosappu Cape Ice Floes*; *The Late Autumn Hidaka Mountains*; *The Winter Flatlands*; *Desiccated Oaks* . . . But one little sketch gave me particular pause. Written in small text, the title was *Portrait of Matakichi Hiro*.

Once the Asahinas had finished their week at a lodge at the foot of Denali, they paid me a visit at my home in Fairbanks. The elderly couple seemed very satisfied to have seen the autumn leaves, fresh snow *and* the aurora borealis all in the space of a single short trip.

I'll never forget what Dr Asahina's wife told me then: 'If my brother was alive, I'm sure he'd have wanted to come to Alaska.'

The Years Go By

This June I held a photo exhibition in Tokyo. As I spend most of the year in Alaska, it was a great opportunity to catch up with people. A childhood friend was there. It had been twenty-five years. Seeing her really took me back. She's running a sushi restaurant with her husband and seems as energetic as ever. I also met for the first time in ages with T's mother.

It's been eighteen years since I found out about T. He and I were just twenty and had been close friends since middle school. I was on the overnight train home after finishing summer camp at Mount Tanigawa when I opened the newspaper and was puzzled to find a photo of his face inside. I had a bad feeling right away: T had come over to my house just ten days earlier to borrow a camera and an ice axe.

'Don't you dare break my camera,' I seem to recall telling him half-jokingly as we parted.

The article described how a party of three from Chiba University that included T had been caught up in a disaster. I'll never forget how long the remainder of my ride to Ueno Station seemed that night.

First thing the following morning, I set off with some friends for Shinshu. While waiting at the local police station, I was kept busy making various phone calls. Through the open window, the radiant sea of summer grass rippling in the breeze caught my eye. It was an awful moment and yet another me stood apart and gazed captivated at the scenery outside. I felt certain that many years later I would remember this sea of summer grass. Because that was when I learned for certain that T was gone.

I saw his mother at the site of the disaster. She had cared for me like a second mother ever since I was practically a child. Even staring at the utterly transformed body of T, she sustained this role. Not showing any tears, she gave me a kindly smile and told me, 'I want you to get twice as much out of life to make up for my boy.' In so doing, she reversed our positions, making me the one who needed repeated consoling. Although T and the ice axe were both piteously broken, my camera had remained somehow unscathed.

In retrospect, that event was like a full stop that punctuated the end of my youth. I searched incessantly for some definitive conclusion to draw from T's death. I needed to find one if I was going to move forward. A year passed until the answer came to me one day. It wasn't anything especially remarkable. Just the strong desire to make it through by doing what I loved. In a roundabout way, T's death brought me to the distinct realization that I was alive in the present. Unconsciously, I had come full circle to what his mother had asked of me that day at the site of the accident.

I had visited Alaska at the age of nineteen. Now it swelled up rapidly inside me. Come what may, I knew that I had to go back there. I wanted to take part in that ludicrously vast wilderness.

When I went back to my college campus, I realized that I no longer belonged there. Students chatting as they carried tennis rackets. Students giving inflammatory speeches in front of signboards. The all too familiar milieu now seemed like a different world to me. I had no plans for the future; all I knew was that I had to get away from there.

I decided to pursue a career in photography and flew again to Alaska. In a flash, thirteen years passed and here I am putting down roots in this land. I've been running non-stop ever since T's death.

Every time I return to Japan, I make sure to visit T's mother. His room has been left just as it was, and I feel as though I am returning to the distant past. His aging mother talks to me as she did long ago and restores me to the boy I was in middle school. But we almost never bring up our memories of T.

The day T's mother came to my exhibition, I felt as though she had grown younger. While we sat in chairs and had a leisurely talk for the first time in years, she suddenly began to regale me with memories of T as though a dam had burst inside her. A bubble seemed to form around us, sealing us off from the rest of the spacious venue.

'Ever since you went off to Alaska, it has felt to me like my boy was traveling along with you . . .'

I probably would have gone off to Alaska whether T had died or not. But would I have taken it up as my subject with the same strength of purpose? And such change would not have been reserved exclusively for me; he would have significantly altered the lives of others around him too. The death of an irreplaceable person often endows a certain power to those they leave behind.

While looking at T's mom, it occurred to me that I had ultimately never seen her shed a tear. In this very absence of tears I seemed to glimpse her sadness, the profound sadness I could never hope to fathom of a mother who has lost a child.

'I started playing table tennis recently,' she told me with eyes shining like a young girl, though she was nearly seventy. I recalled a faded photo she had once shown me of her fitted out for mountain climbing when she was still a student. For some reason, an image of her playing table tennis combined with that photo in my mind.

T's long-bedridden grandmother had passed away the previous year. His mother seems to have been stuck at home for many years caring for the woman. All manner of burdens were steadily lifting away from her.

'Why don't we have a table tennis match sometime?' I suggested. She nodded happily. And I really meant it; I would love to face off with T's mom someday.

Ocean Currents

Climbing Franklin Hill, I turn left on 2nd Street and arrive at Observatory Books.

This small city, Juneau, the capital of Alaska, is just covered in hills. After gold was found in a nearby valley during the Gold Rush of the late nineteenth century, it was built on a meagre set of slopes just beyond fjords, as if groveling before the range of sheer coastal mountains that loom over it.

Nowhere in America will you find a state capital so beautiful – or so isolated. Juneau still lacks a connecting road; the only transportation is either by plane or boat. From the air you can see that the mountains host a massive icefield, with one glacier that flows toward the city, while dense primeval forest coats the lower peaks and slopes. This terrain of ice and trees is created by annual rainfall of some one hundred and sixty inches due to moist ocean air hitting the coastal mountains. The Kuroshio – or Black Current – brings this moist air as it circulates in a great arc across the northern Pacific Ocean all the way from Japan, along the Aleutians and into southern Alaska.

The Tlingit and Haida developed totem pole cultures in this secluded region, cut off by deep forests, vast icefields and precipitous mountains, and I have long wondered where these peoples came from. Distinct from both the Inuit of the Arctic coast and the Athabascans of the interior, they occupy a unique position among Alaska Natives, remaining shrouded in mystery.

The door to Observatory Books is open; the old dog lies in the entrance as usual. Completely deaf, it never thinks to budge when customers enter and will sometimes cut obliviously across the road as though the honking of cars were just some distant breeze.

'That's why I can't let this dog out of my sight,' Dee the old lady proprietress once told me.

'Hi, Dee!' I greet her now.

'Oh, long time no see . . .' she says. 'You remember that book about totem poles you came looking for the other day? I still don't know what I did with it. It's a real find, that one.'

'Don't worry about it. I just came to browse for a bit.'

Whenever I travel to Juneau, I find myself climbing Franklin without even meaning to; I just can't help stopping by Observatory Books. It seems I still haven't beaten my addiction to used bookstores from my days in Tokyo. I have been known to frequent the used-bookstore districts in both Waseda, where my mother's family lived, and Kanda, a favorite haunt of mine that I discovered in college.

Ever since I settled in Alaska, I've derived great pleasure from in seeking out aged volumes that take the state as their theme. A more-than-century-old travelogue about an Inuit village. A Brooks Range expeditionary chronicle from the dawn of exploration. A collection of faded Gold Rush photographs. I've tracked down innumerable classics with the word 'Alaska' in the title, each speaking in the voices of this land's erstwhile inhabitants.

But my obsession with such venerable tomes isn't the only thing that keeps bringing me back to Observatory; it's also Dee herself. I've never known anyone who relishes the job of running a used bookstore so much.

'You really seem to like this, Dee,' I once told her.

'I do – I love Alaskan history!' she replied. 'Especially the pre-1867 period, before America bought the land from Russia.'

And indeed, Dee's knowledge of Alaskan history is incredible. Names and dates stream out of her like you're talking to an encyclopedia. Forever admiring of her, I once asked how she retained so much. For some reason she seemed embarrassed by the question.

'About the world today, I forget important things; but about Alaskan history, I remember even the most boring trivia.'

The old lady has several amusing quirks. One is her raconteur-like delivery, with every word and gesture so laugh-out-loud funny it's like you're watching an American comedy classic. The other is her inability to stop talking once she gets going. You have to be extremely careful what question you ask her if you're in any kind of a hurry or you may forfeit your opportunity to leave.

Patrons are eligible for a ten per cent discount on any book purchased at Observatory if their job happens to be the same as that of any of Dee's daughters. One of her daughters works for a newspaper company, so by stretching the definition of journalist she has managed to squeeze me into the rebate. Incidentally, the other professions blessed with this perquisite are dancers, actors and neophyte lawyers.

'I've got a fascinating map here. Want to take a look?' Everyone is inspired by something; for old Dee it has always been maps. They are her specialty, particularly antique maps from an age when the unknown still stretched vast upon the world, and Observatory carries a large collection of such cartographic curios in addition to its used books.

'I'm captivated by the history of maps ultimately because I'm interested in people,' Dee explained to me on a previous visit. 'Maps teach us how we came to grasp the world piece by piece.'

Dee now takes out a map, spreads it out on the table and covers it with a protective sheet of clear plastic. I see a chart of the North Pacific, including Japan and Alaska, which she tells me was produced in the seventeenth century. More like an illustration than a modern map, it is wanting in accuracy, with continents and islands only impressionistically located. On closer inspection, I make out French text, suggesting it was drawn up in Europe.

'Had any Japanese person sailed the North Pacific more than three hundred years ago?' Dee asks. 'And how were your map-making skills back then?'

'Um, I don't know for sure but I doubt that any of us went on a voyage like that,' I say. 'And we didn't have the technology to make maps yet.'

Evidently satisfied by my response, Dee begins to pontificate on the mystery of this map.

'This is a reproduction of a map obtained by a Westerner who went to Japan in the 1600s. He was shown the map by your imperial family and took it back home to Europe to rework it. That is to say, the original was in seventeenth-century Japan. The puzzle is how such a map could have ended up there when map-making was undeveloped, nor had any Japanese sailed the North Pacific.'

This is how she always launches into her talks. And as always, I am drawn along with her before I know it into the allure of antiquarian maps. The old lady's extensive knowledge may be what keeps Observatory in business as much as its inventory of books.

After a thorough perusal of the shelves, I sit on the chair in front of Dee's desk. When I have time to spare, I love to lounge here and while away the hours listening to her tales. Even as the topic meanders in every possible direction, her understanding of Alaskan history leaves me in awe.

I recall a certain matter that I've long been wanting to look into and wonder if I've finally hit upon something that will stump Dee. It concerns an anecdote, caught in the threads of my memory, that a friend once shared with me – the kind of stirring adventure that transports you right back to childhood. I am referring to the tale of a ghost ship.

From the eighteenth century through the nineteenth century, many whaling vessels and other sorts of ships traveled through the Bering Sea to the Arctic Ocean. Untold numbers met disaster along the way. A common fate was for them to be pincered and beached by sea ice as pieces of it collided and swelled with the approach of winter, solidifying into icefields. Any ship lifted onto the frozen ocean surface in this way would then be carried on ceaseless Arctic currents, continuing their voyage even to this day. These ghost ships pass every decade or two through waters near coastal Inuit villages, from which residents gather on the shore to catch a glimpse of this uncanny sight, warning children never to approach.

It was one such story that my friend heard from an Inuit elder. The question is, could it possibly be true? I suddenly can't resist asking Dee.

'Yes, the name of that ship is the SS *Baychimo*,' she tells me. 'I believe it was a nineteenth-century whaler. One of our older albums should have a photo of it off the coast of Nome perhaps seventy or eighty years ago. Let me go take a look.'

Dee disappears into the back room and instantly emerges with an armload of photo albums.

'These were taken by a white person who was living in Nome at the time. Most capture the Inuit way of life such as it was then, but I believe a shot of the *Baychimo* is in there too. Should be a small photo about the size of a playing card. It shows the ghost ship in the offing all covered in ice.'

I'm overcome with wonder as we turn the pages of one of the weathered albums together. Irrespective of the people featured or the quality of the shots, any collection of photos capturing

Alaska in the 1920s and 30s is a rare treasure indeed. All the more so if the photographer abided in Inuit society. Dee collects these visions of life from lost eras, in addition to maps and books, for her own personal enjoyment.

As I flip through the album with anticipation, one of the photos gives me pause. It shows a couple along with a small airplane. The face of the man is oddly familiar.

'That's Charles Lindbergh. This is when he flew to Alaska with his wife after coming to world fame for completing his transatlantic flight.'

I had no idea that Lindbergh visited Alaska. And to think that such a priceless image was tucked away in this album all these years. But we cannot seem to find the photo of the ghost ship, so we divide up the albums and begin to search separately.

'It's really not much of a photo, just a ship off the coast. You're liable to miss it if you don't look carefully. But I just know it was covered in ice . . .'

Our work is interrupted whenever a customer enters the shop. By the time we've scoured the same stack of albums several times, nearly an hour has elapsed. Dee suggests that the photo may have gotten mixed up somewhere else and hauls out a mountain of other albums from the back room, but I'm feeling kind of tired and lie down on the couch.

The Observatory couch is a cushy antique surrounded by bookshelves in the middle of the shop; its presence adds to the cozy sense that you are in someone's living room. The battered couch, the books piled hither and thither, the old dog sprawled on the floor. This ambiance of perfect chaos may be the secret to the bookshop's greatness. There is no expectation here that you buy the books; you are free to just plump yourself onto the couch and read. Dee even seems to prefer the kind of customer who does so.

Stricken now with full-on sleepiness, I find myself slipping into a reverie on the couch, thinking of the SS *Baychimo*. Hordes of ghost ships sealed in ice, not a soul onboard, continuing their century-long voyage. And, yes, the Arctic currents that carry them . . . Eyes shut in repose, I can almost see the dreamlike spectacle before me.

So that whaling vessel shipwrecked in the nineteenth century was the SS *Baychimo*. I recall another tale from the period. In 1839, an American whaling vessel sailing the North Pacific spotted a drifting ship of wholly unfamiliar make. Upon approaching, the whaling crew found seven men curled up barely alive. This would turn out to be a sailboat that had been caught in a storm, carried away from the shores of Edo-era Japan by the Kuroshio and put out to open sea.

The *Chojamaru* had left port in Toyama on the Sea of Japan on April 29th in the ninth year of the Tenpo emperor's reign (1838). Nine sailors served onboard under fifty-year-old Captain Heishiro. Their names and ages were Hachizaemon (fifty), Hachizaemon (same name, forty-seven), Zenuemon (forty-two), Tasaburo (forty), Rokusaburo (thirty-one), Jirokichi (twenty-six), Gosaburo (twenty-five), Shichizaemon (twenty-three) and Kinzo (eighteen). Freighted with rice and bound for Osaka, the *Chojamaru* was just one of many ships that crisscrossed Japan's coastal waters transporting goods and supplies under the jurisdiction of the Edo shogunate regime.

It arrived in Osaka at the end of May, then set sail with a new cargo of cotton and sugar on a return course to the Sea of Japan, this time bound for Echigo (present-day Niigata) before making its way by mid-August to Matsumae in the land of Ezo (present-day Hokkaido), all without incident. But one day during the month that the crew spent in Matsumae preparing for their next journey, the steersman Hachizaemon announced his resignation, having bad premonitions about their upcoming voyage between the Straits of Tsugaru and along the eastern coast to Edo (present-day Tokyo). So he was replaced at the helm by a man named Kinroku who was experienced in navigating these treacherous waters.

The next complication arose at the end of September. After the *Chojamaru* had been loaded up in Hakodate with a large freight of kelp and was making its way straight down the coast for Sendai, the ship was found in want of repairs and they were forced to dock in Tanohama (present-day Iwate). During the two weeks that it took to service the *Chojamaru*, Buddhist priests and Shinto shrine maidens came in succession to offer their blessings for the crew's safe voyage. But one shrine maiden who arrived later than the rest told them something strange: she claimed to have had a vision of disaster befalling the ship between the dates of November 23rd and 24th. Being Buddhists, however, the sailors doubted the prophecy and merely laughed at her.

Then the *Chojamaru* was held up in Sendai for another two weeks due to rough weather, making it precisely November 23rd when the skies cleared at last. The ship left port at 8am that day and was exiting the mouth of the bay some two hours later when the red wind came upon them, an ominous force said to redden the ocean's surface where it blows and to never return a ship to shore. The sailors worked furiously to re-hoist the sail, as a great gale pushed the *Chojamaru* further and further into the offing, until one of the ropes among the rigging snapped. Control of the ship was now lost, and it drifted gradually out to open sea, until by day on the 25th even the peak of Kinkasan island, the last speck of land, vanished over the watery horizon.

The sailors could not hope to guess where they were being taken but felt certain to a man that they would never see home again. Not knowing whether there were any foreign lands here at the ends of the oceans or how long they might expect to survive, all the despairing crew could do was relinquish their fates to the current and float along to whatever destination awaited.

As November turned to December, the temperature dropped and snow began to fall. Their stores of rice and water depleted, and themselves emaciated to skin and bone, the sailors spent each day praying to the buddhas as they strayed through the unknown. When the new year arrived, Gosaburo and Zenuemon died. Next steersman Kinroku threw himself into the sea. The seven remaining sailors waited for their turns, fending off starvation on a diet of just kelp and rainwater.

One morning in April 1839, some mountain-like thing emerged from the horizon. The sailors could hardly move but they all watched as the giant boat approached. Their fear of this bizarre ship like none any had laid eyes upon before was overpowered by the keenness of their thirst. If they were going to be killed, they decided, they'd like to drink down bucketloads of water first.

Onboard the floating monolith were foreign men in peculiar clothes. After circling in the proximity of the *Chojamaru* several times, the ship dispatched a small boat and closed in. Incapable of rising to their feet, the sailors had to somehow face these aliens coming aboard. And so it was that the isolated civilization of Edo-period Japan made wordless contact with the world.

The *Chojamaru* had encountered an American whaler called the *James Loper*. The seven Japanese sailors changed into fine kimono that they had set aside and were assisted aboard. Their four months adrift had come to an end.

After being forcibly dragged away from a homeland sealed up for hundreds of years by the closed-island policy of the Edo shogunate, these men were now traveling the world, passing from one exotic ship to the next as they visited Hawaii, Kamchatka and finally Sitka, the capital of Russian-controlled Alaska. Then in March of 1843, a Russian vessel embarked from Sitka bound for Etrof (present-day Iturup) under orders from the czar to take the seven castaways home.

A two-month voyage later – and four years after the mishap that had sent them off course – the sailors made it back to Japan after all. But they were immediately labeled criminals, as was standard under shogunate rule for anyone who had set foot on foreign soil, and imprisoned in Edo for interrogations. Although such questioning was infamous for being wide-ranging and drawn-out, it seems that what the castaways had seen was especially stimulating to the shogunate scholars in charge, in their great hunger for outside knowledge after Japan's long self-enclosure, because it would be another three years before the crew were allowed to return to their respective hometowns.

Among the recorded testimonies, the contributions of young Jirokichi were particularly noteworthy. For he not only had a subtle and receptive mind that allowed him to soak up and recall every experience in detail, but he also possessed a talent for drawing from memory. His illustrations of the scenery in Sitka and of its indigenous peoples vividly conjure the Alaska of that period.

In the chronicle of the *Chojamaru*, what interests me more than either the sailors' accounts or the character of Jirokichi is the Kuroshio that instigated the whole misadventure, circulating through the North Pacific since time out of mind, flowing perpetually round and round as if in search of a way out. The Kuroshio is fed by the current that flows northward from the waters near easternmost Japan. When part of this splits off toward the Bering Sea, the rest becomes the main current and traces the southern coast of Alaska before arcing southward to British Columbia. One branching current subsequently travels to eastern Hawaii and gradually disperses. Another current, however, sustains the Kuroshio southward in the direction of the equator, before proceeding to Guam and Taiwan and at last passing northward again through the waters east of Japan.

I wonder how many Japanese ships in all of history have lost their rudder or sail and been swept off by the forceful currents of the Kuroshio, never to be heard of again. Although most were likely lost at sea, a few might have been fortunate enough to wash up with their crew still living on the shores of Kamchatka, the Aleutians or even southern Alaska.

Official records show that a portion of lost Japanese ships in the years prior to the *Chojamaru*'s 1839 misfortune did indeed find their way to Alaska and neighboring regions:

1782: Aleutians
1805: Sitka
1813: At sea 49° N 131° W
1815: At sea 32° N 166° W
1820: Point Adams
1833: Cape Flattery
1862: Attu
1871: Adak

One can only speculate as to how many Japanese mariners made it to land only to die at the hands of the local indigenous people. But a very lucky few who stepped ashore on the Alaskan coast may have gone without mortal injury and survived. These would have surely accepted their fate, given up on ever returning home and joined whichever society they encountered in that strange realm. In this way, such castaways would have contributed fresh blood to the existing cultures. How far back might their history go?

Here the unforgettable words a Tlingit friend once blurted to me become important.

'The blood of the Japanese may be mixed with ours. There is story from our oral tradition that allows us to imagine so.'

The Tlingit and Haida were maritime peoples who once formed totem-pole-building civilizations that extended from present-day Southeast Alaska to British Columbia. It is unlikely that they ever knew famine or that any indigenous peoples in North America since the dawn of history were more blessed with natural abundance. All they had to do was head out to sea, which was teeming with catch from salmon, halibut and herring to seals and northern sea lions, or hike into the forests to hunt deer and gather tree nuts. Meanwhile, warm ocean currents guaranteed a mild seaside climate throughout the year. It was the search for more plentiful ecosystems that is said to have originally brought these peoples' ancestors from the interior, climbing through the steep valleys of the Coast Mountains and following rivers downstream on their incremental migration to this coastal region.

A resource-rich life without fear of famine is no doubt what gave the Haida and Tlingit enough leisure time to develop cultural products of high artistic sophistication, including totem poles, paintings and textiles. But was this the only factor? Into their exceedingly isolated world, cut off and divided from the outside by deep forests and vast glaciers, might there not have been visitors from across the ocean possessed of entirely distinct cultures? One must wonder especially about the provenance of the Haida's and Tlingit's strict ethical codes, analogues of which are not to be found among their Alaskan Native neighbors, whether Athabascan or Inuit.

The following story told by a Tlingit elder has been left for posterity. Here it is as related by my friend:

> Once upon a time, people were carried from out of the sea and made landfall at Dall Island, off the southwestern coast of Prince of Wales Island. Those people, called Wudisháni.át [which apparently means some kind of very old organism], are said to be the distant ancestors of the Teikweidí clan.

The maritime peoples practiced totem-pole building and organized their lineages into clans, believing that their forebears originated as the incarnation of various animals. From this a complex hierarchical society based on each clan's animal developed, with the wolf and raven being especially central, and the Teikweidí treated as the oldest and most important clan of the Tlingit's wolf moiety. Many elders thought that the foreigners from the sea were ancestors to the Teikweidí and the first people to settle on this coast, meaning that the indigenous of the interior migrated here in search of ocean catch only later. These two groups were then said to have merged before subsequently splitting into the Tlingit and Haida.

If this legend is true, who could these overseas newcomers have been? And in what era would they have arrived?

According to the Tlingit oral tradition of which this tale is a part, the ocean arrivals were split into two groups – each led by one of two sisters. Those led by the younger sister went south to the present-day Queen Charlotte Islands* and became the progenitors of the Haida. Those led by the elder sister remained, merging with the migrants from landlocked regions beyond the mountains, and became the progenitors of the Tlingit. The Teikweidí trace their lineage directly to the elder sister. And when the tribes divided by the two sisters reunited at festivals and funerals, Haida, descendants of the younger sister, had to give up the most powerful seats to the Tlingit, descendants of the elder sister.

This oral tradition lends credence to the possibility that these maritime peoples are related by blood to Asians and suggests an explanation for how the former produced such sophisticated cultures so quickly. And isn't there some chance that they are related specifically to the Japanese? Might there not have been another *Chojamaru* long ago, well before the Edo period, that was snatched away one fateful day by the Kuroshio? Or perhaps this current has been responsible for not just one or two but many *Chojamaru*s, all carried off to unknown worlds.

When I come to, I'm still resting where I was on the sofa at Observatory Books. I've been snoozing here for close to an hour. Dee has transferred the heap of albums to her desk as she continues to search for the photo of the ghost ship *Baychimo*.

'This is so weird . . .' she says. 'I'm just sure it's in one of these albums. The photo is all faded but you can see a ship

---

* The name was officially reverted to Haida Gwaii in 2010.

covered in ice looking small in the distance and the back is labeled *Baychimo*.'

'Don't worry about it,' I tell her. 'If it ever turns up, just let me know. I'll come back to take a look for sure.'

From one of the shelves, I select a book about raven mythology that has long interested me.

'Uh, you're someone who takes photographs, which makes you basically a journalist, so that'll be ten per cent off.'

A mist of rain has begun to fall outside. As I go down the hill on Franklin, I'm musing about the ghost ship, when something I never put much thought into is suddenly illuminated inside me: the beachcombers living along the Alaskan coast. On the several occasions I've spoken to them, they've told me that they like going to the beach after work to walk along the surf at dusk in search of washed-up objects. But it's not just any old flotsam and jetsam that excites them; they seem to prize strange objects that have drifted over from distant and unfamiliar places. I'm told that beachcombing is particularly fun after a storm. The surprising part is that most of the items they find here have come from Japan. Among these, the large round glass floats used by Japanese fisherman are considered especially precious. I can't count the number of times someone has proudly displayed one of these to me. I have always just stared at them with disinterest. Even though there could have been a grand story tucked away inside each one . . .

Raindrops begin to fall. The mist moves lifelike between the trees of the deep forest. It could be snowing on the mountaintop glaciers. As the rain soaks through to my skin, I feel the warm hint of currents that ceaselessly flow from faraway lands.

PART THREE

PART THREE

Midnight Sun

'Don, let's go for a jaunt,' I say. 'We can't miss out on a night like this.'

'Might as well,' Don says with a dispirited nod. 'There's no point obsessing over what happened I guess.'

You can always count on my friend Don Ross the bush pilot to greet the worst with a smile.

Here we are inside the Arctic Circle, on the upper reaches of the Kongakut River where it flows through the Brooks Range. Follow it all the way downstream and you end up at the Arctic Ocean. We're camping along the riverbank, with Don's beloved Cessna 175 parked beside the tents. The landscape around our site would have made quite the painting. And we might have been able to appreciate it more if not for one thing: the Cessna's bent propellor.

Don messed up on the takeoff. Overly front-loaded, the plane plunged its nose into the tundra the moment it started to move. Landings and takeoffs are always fraught with danger when you fly over the Alaskan wilds, where nothing so reliable as a runway is to be found. The conditions of the tundra don't help either. The ground always looks smooth from the air, then you make your approach and see all the bumps; these ensure that landings are a tense affair until the plane has come to a stop. A single stone or the slightest hollow can be fatal.

The mishap with the Cessna was over in an instant. Don then stood tapping the propeller with a hammer to relieve stress more than anything, exchanging looks with me now and again. We both knew there was no way we were flying. Which meant we were stranded – in the northernmost mountains of Alaska no less. Even the closest Athabascan village was on the other side of the Brooks Range, a full sixty miles away. We had managed to communicate our predicament via distress signal only to be told that a new propellor wouldn't arrive from Fairbanks for a week. We had no clue whether the engine would turn out to be damaged, nor how much Don would have to pay for repairs.

Our one consolation was when the thick fog that had persisted for days cleared, making for a lovely night. This left us torn as to whether to curl up in our sleeping bags and go to sleep or climb the mountain and give up on having a night at all. It was the season of the midnight sun, angling its rays from the horizon, never setting.

Having come to a decision now at last, we put coffee and trail snacks in our light backpacks, leave all our worries at basecamp and climb the night mountain.

We have been traveling the Eastern Brooks Range in search of caribou herds. Recording their migrations through the Arctic is a major theme of my work. For I seek primeval nature that is wild in the true meaning of that word.

The buffalo that once covered the plains of North America are no more to be seen. Awe-inspiring landscapes redolent of prehistoric times have all been consigned to legend. This is to be expected, with modernity already far behind us as we approach a new era in the twenty-first century, like something out of science fiction. And yet one spectacle from the kind of nature that we have lost remains in the world of deepest north: the great herds of caribou who wander the wilds of the Arctic Circle enveloped in a white veil.

I have followed the roaming caribou as though guided down a time tunnel. On this journey for the past decade, Don has been the ideal partner. It's not just his dependability as a pilot. More important for me is that he views the wilderness of Alaska in much the same way I do.

Given his bohemian lifestyle today, I struggle to picture him as the elite American Air Force pilot he once was. I'm not clear why he threw away that status to become a humble Alaskan bush pilot. In the winter, he now also delivers supplies to African refugee camps, a long-held dream of his.

I like Don. He has that kind of gentleness possessed by those who have stepped down from another life. We have seen so many landscapes together.

It must have been five years ago that we were flying along the shore of the Arctic Ocean when we came across a massive herd of caribou just smothering the tundra. As we marveled in wonder at the scene of tens of thousands of these animals traversing an untrammeled land as yet beyond humanity's grasp, something Don muttered in the pilot's seat beside me was picked up by the mic and came in over my headphones.

'The world we're looking down on right now is just as it was a thousand, no ten thousand years ago.'

On the tundra one bright polar night, we also watched with bated breath another scene unchanged since ancient times: that of a wolf hunting a pack of caribou. Both of us are always moved by signs of a nature that breathes not for humans nor for anything else but for the sake of its own being.

While we walk, Don hardly speaks; his mind seems to be on the propellor after all. Soon we reach a point where we must cross the Kongakut River. Fording a river of the Far North is always dangerous. Even if the water isn't deep, the icy cold is terrifying. Because once you start crossing, you can't pause or turn back. At the stiffening pain, I feel like I'm going to lose my balance in the rapids.

Once we've waded to the other side and begin to climb an alpine tundra slope, we spot patches of flowers here and there and hear the guttural cluck of a rock ptarmigan out of sight. The low sun of polar summer, hidden when we were in the valley, reveals itself as we gain altitude, bathing us in soft light.

We decide to sit down in a field of flowers for a short rest. Having flown all day, Don stretches out and closes his eyes. Among the small flowers of the deep north swaying in the breeze walks a golden plover that has finished nesting.

It's only July but I wonder if the bird is already preparing to return south.

'Hey, Michio,' Don calls to me out of the blue. 'What do you suppose this place will look like in a hundred years?'

It's times like these that tell me his perspective on the Alaskan wilderness is much like mine.

As we climb further, the mountain abruptly opens into a cirque formation and we find a meadow of hare's-tail cottongrass extending in front of us. The feathery white puffs of their flowers turn gold under the midnight sun, shining like myriad treasures. Then, gazing around us in a trance, what do we see appearing one after the next over the shoulder of a distant mountain but little specks of caribou. Presently this swatch of dots on the ridge becomes a thick line, then a black band that covers the mountainside and begins to head straight for us.

Alarmed, we take off at a run and dive for cover into the cottongrass. Noisily panting out white breath, we unsling our packs and lie where we are in the summer grass. The fragrant scent of summer-tundra soil. The cerulean sky of a polar night stretching endlessly. Thoughts clear from my mind and, keeping still, I feel as though droves of caribou are passing silently over us.

The failed takeoff could mean a significant financial loss for my solitary friend Don. But if we were flying safely, we wouldn't be here right now.

'It's a gift,' says Don.

A rumbling sound gradually swells around us. Soon we are encompassed within the sea of golden shining cottongrass by a herd of caribou thousands strong.

Early Spring

The soft April breeze slowly loosens the taut air of winter and the emotions of those who have endured that long dark season. Why is it that the warmth of the sun and the signs of spring bring us happiness, if only fleetingly?

Taking a moment to catch my breath, I loosen the backpack digging into my shoulders and allow the pleasant early-spring breeze to stroke my sweaty skin. Then I remove my sunglasses and survey the area, my eyes dazzled by snow glare.

'The snow really is deep this year,' I say.

'It sure is,' John replies. 'I just hope we can find him before the sun goes down.'

The snow compacts beneath John's snowshoes as he treads through it, then stops and turns on the instrument hanging from his neck, holding the antenna as high as he can. Beep, beep, beep . . . The volume changes as he moves the antenna around. The bear is definitely in this valley.

We are on a mountain in a suburb of Fairbanks, the city I call home. Guided by the beeping of the receiver, we wander between trunks of silver birch and spruce from forest to forest. Our feet catch frequently in the snow, so deep that without snowshoes we would sink in up to our chests.

We are a hardy team of six if you count our leader John, all of us from the Alaska Department of Fish and Game, searching in the mountains of early spring for the den of a hibernating black bear. As part of a study into the range of black bears, our job is to replace the tracking collar installed when the bear was captured this summer before the batteries, which dwindle over winter, completely run out.

Three days ago, we circled over these mountains in a small airplane equipped with a special antenna and ascertained the bear's general whereabouts. But there was no telling if we would precisely locate him in the valleys of this vast mountain until we actually attempted to find him on the ground. An added complication was that the area had seen its largest snowfall in decades.

At this time of year, bears are not hibernating in the true sense of that word. Rather than being in a state of suspended animation with reduced metabolism like the Arctic ground squirrel, they merely doze. A pregnant sow will give birth in her winter den, and any bear will wake up quickly if danger approaches. It is well known that bears store up fat for the winter, but I still wonder by what specific mechanism they can survive without eating anything for six whole months.

When traveling through the Alaskan wilderness, you always sense the presence of bears out there somewhere, even if you don't encounter them. This is a true luxury in our world today. For the presence of bears arouses a feeling of primal tension forgotten by humankind. If bears disappeared from this land and we could sleep fearlessly in our camps at night, what a boring kind of nature it would be. April is the time of year when you first sense the proximity of bears beneath the snow without seeing them.

Although spring has begun, the daylight hours remain short and dusk is already approaching. We have been walking continuously for close to six hours now and are growing impatient. Then, at just after four o'clock, the receiver starts to beep with the greatest intensity yet.

'Guys,' John hisses, 'he's around here!'

Our voices drop instantly to a whisper. The bear should be under the snow within a ten-yard radius. After leaning our backpacks against the trunk of a silver birch, we remove our snowshoes, take a single step and immediately sink in up to our waists. I can feel the granular spring snow soaking into my body.

In a normal year when the snow is not so deep, we would have found his little breathing holes by carefully scanning the snow's surface. Now we search around nervously for signs of anything vaguely resembling such perforations. Nervous because we could without knowing be standing directly atop a sleeping bear.

Time is running short. Each of us grabs a shovel and we begin to dig into the surrounding snow. We are incredibly close but somehow can't quite find him. An hour passes. In the snow beside a birch a small hole suddenly opens to a depth of six feet. Our voices grow even quieter.

'Steve, go take a peek inside!' John says.

This is always Steve's job, the poor guy. We watch him below us with great trepidation. No sooner has he turned on his flashlight and brought his face close to the hole than he recoils back.

'What's the matter?'

'I was almost nose-to-nose with him,' says Steve. 'Felt his breath on my face.'

We set to work swiftly. A syringe of anesthetic is attached to a long pole. This time it's John who lowers himself to the hole. The bear has retreated to the back of his den. We rapidly slide the pole in, test the syringe and cover the entrance with a sleeping bag. This last measure – more reassuring than likely to be effective – is to prevent the furious bear from leaping out at us. It's quite the primitive technique.

Five minutes pass.

'Michio, go take a peek inside!'

I poke my head into the hole and warily shine my light. Twigs neatly bed the floor of a den, at the back of which crouches a black boulder-like mass. Incredible that bears wait unmoving for six months in such tiny spaces.

Steve sticks his upper body into the hole and attempts to shift the bear toward the entrance but gets stuck on a tree root and flails his legs in the air trying to free himself. We burst out laughing even as Steve remains dead serious, face to face with a bear that has been anesthetized (we hope). We all tug on

Steve's legs and after some effort manage to pull him out, now covered in snow.

The bear is three years old. This would have been his first time holing up alone over the winter, after parting with his mother. We pull the young bear out onto the snow; there he breaths softly, sound asleep. With some thirty minutes remaining until the anesthetic wears off, the process of replacing the transmitter proceeds steadily.

I sit down beside the bear and stroke his coarse fur, testing the texture of each hair. His clean and well-groomed coat is much more handsome in a wild kind of way than one might imagine. I put my palm to his lips, feeling the warmth of his faint breath, then try gently inserting my index finger into his mouth. My fingertip is enveloped in the bear's body heat. When I bury my face in his soft belly, his pungent aroma fills my nostrils and the warmth of his skin spreads across my face. I try to store this remote and savage smell in my memory as though breathing deeply with my mind.

By the time John has taken a blood sample for the study and the six of us have lifted the bear up to measure his bodyweight, our time is up. His breath becomes increasingly disturbed. He is starting to rouse himself from the drug.

Putting the bear back in his den is a major operation. We must restore him to his reclusive slumbers as though nothing has happened. Together we support his enormous four-hundred-and-fifty-pound body while laying him in his original position, before covering the entrance to his burrow with dead wood and meticulously layering on snow. Soon the six-foot hole we dug in the snow is neatly buried and surfaced.

I narrow my eyes to scan the distant mountain skyline. Could that dot be a house standing there all alone? Someone is actually living out there. I want to let them know: beneath a spruce tree that I'm sure you can see from the window of your house, a bear is hibernating in his lair. Soon he's bound to feel the signs of spring and lumber out from beneath the snow . . .

As we descend the mountain at dusk, I glance back one last time at the site of the bear's burrow. All I see now is snow and a lone tree, a patch of landscape indistinguishable from the surround. The figure I have so recently observed, that three-year-old bear crouching unmoving in his lair as he waits for spring, is burned into my memory. He exudes an even fiercer will to live than any bear roaming the summer wilds. Following the snowy path, I am filled with a kind of exultation that makes me want to scream aloud.

Spring is on its way to Alaska.

Ruth Glacier

I hear an avalanche, perhaps an ice wall collapsing somewhere. The wave-like roar soon subsides, to be followed by the sound of numerous stones scattering down a rockface. This too fades into the darkness. The taut tranquility of a night glacier.

Countless stars twinkle in the firmament. The silence of the cosmos blankets me. Why does Orion look so big in Alaska's night sky? In the upper left of the constellation is Betelgeuse; in its lower right is Rigel. Extend the ladle of the Big Dipper five times to find the North Star . . . This is the domain of the stars that I memorized in childhood rumination. And yet, they say that Polaris will change places in some twelve thousand years with another star, which will then become the North Star. All life travels endlessly over the horizon of eternity; not even the stars remain fixed.

The starlight in the heavens seems almost close enough to reach out and touch. They say that it is from tens of thousands to hundreds of millions of years ago and has only just arrived. Since each of the innumerable stars emits its light from a different number of light-years away, tilting your eyes to the night sky is to take in the staggering history of the universe in a single instant. But even if we grasp this in words, we are not capable of understanding it truly and can only prostrate ourselves before something.

As I remain focused on the northern sky, a streak of blue light emerges and soon begins to shimmer and sway. I have been waiting with prayerful heart; now I call the children out from the lodge.

We are at the head of the Ruth Glacier that stretches across the southern face of the Alaska Range. Although Denali held the fading light of sunset to the last, it is now just a black silhouette, blending with the mountain range that surrounds us, a colossal amphitheater of snow, ice and rock constructed by nature. The moonlight raises a blue glow from the icy overhang of the rockfaces; the planetarium-like starry sky presses so close you feel as though you could fly right up into it.

For many years, whenever March arrived, I would visit Ruth Glacier to take pictures of the northern lights. Here awaited a mysterious space where I could enter into dialogue with the universe. Spending the night atop this great monolith of ice, surrounded by mountains ten to twenty thousand feet tall, I gazed at cold flame dancing in a dark sky like a thing alive. In these moments, I felt like the lone audience for a drama of the cosmos on nature's grand stage. Over time, I came to wish that I could share the experience with someone. And I began to wonder what powerful memory would have remained with me if I had witnessed such a scene as a child when the receptivity of my mind was still sharp. It wouldn't have mattered whether the northern lights even appeared. How wonderful it would be to spend the night atop the glacier with my younger self and show him those stars that seemed to fall like rain amid the breathtaking void.

A small uninhabited cabin here suggested to me that I might in a certain sense make that vision a reality. What if I could bring Japanese children to Ruth Glacier? The late great mountain bush pilot Don Sheldon had loved the view so much that he built the cabin on a rocky outcrop over the icefield. The small area surrounding it represented the only safe zone on a glacier filled with all manner of hazards, from avalanches to the many deep-mouthed crevasses. Thanks to this arrangement, you can pitch tent and camp in the snow, knowing that there is always a cabin to retreat into if anything untoward happens. Ultimately, I consulted with Don Sheldon's widow about my idea and obtained her permission to use the cabin each year.

So in spring of last year, I collaborated with an acquaintance from my student days to fly out eleven children ranging from elementary- to high-school age. Once they were here in Alaska, we took them aboard a small fleet of Cessnas, passing close between the rock and ice walls of an indomitable glacier, landed on the deep freshly fallen snow, plowed ourselves a path and arrived here at the cabin. Then we set them loose upon the vast glacier, watching them transition from being overwhelmed and nervous to gradually seeming at one with the scenery.

'My girl is a tough one to handle,' a carpenter friend of mine has cautioned me. 'I'm counting on you.'

The daughter he speaks of, a high-schooler I will call J, has gotten herself covered in snow as she struggles with cross-country skis, her first time. According to her father, she is going through a rebellious phase that just won't end.

K, like a military general of a boy, immediately takes charge of some elementary-school students he has just met and launches an uproarious sumo tournament atop the glacier. Do these rascals even realize what spectacular scenery they're in? I worry for moment, but then kids will be kids after all.

One middle-schooler named T who seems exceedingly sensible stands apart from the boisterous fray. T attends a college prep school and has the air of one who has fought his way through brutal examinations. I'm concerned whether he is truly enjoying this trip.

Camp life in the wintertime begins with the melting of snow to make water. You must learn to efficiently use the scarce supply available for all dishwashing, cooking and drinking needs. Kids complain at first about little specks on their dishes; later they stop caring and you will find them devouring the curry with rice or whatever else is served upon them.

While we do have tents, the temperature inside is no different from that outside. In the morning, after sleeping in minus-twenty-degree air, how profoundly grateful the kids must be for the fire of the cabin's woodburning stove. Gradually they are returning to nature from their coddled urban lives. In this place devoid of the regular conveniences, what matters most is to stay alive by eating, sleeping and keeping as warm as you can. Taking pause to attend to the truly simple has to be good for them, even if it's only for a week.

Today the sky has cleared at last.

'The northern lights might come out tonight,' I announce.

'No way. How can you tell?' asks a thoroughly suntanned child.

'You just sort of know from, like, the smell of the aurora.'

I reply with some off-the-cuff silliness while inwardly I yearn for the night as if for something sacred. The Cessnas are coming tomorrow and we will have to descend from the mountains.

The aurora begins to flicker, slowly changing shape as it dances across the night sky high above the glacier. The children leap out of the cabin and shriek as they look up. Some try to take photos. Others lie down on the snow. J the high-schooler walks around on the snow nonstop with skyward eyes, as though unsure what else to do with herself.

'It's the northern lights – I'm really seeing them,' she marvels. 'Before we came, I couldn't imagine what we'd do for a whole week in a place without television or anything, but once we got here I never had thoughts like that again . . .'

T the middle-schooler remains separate from the exuberant children, sitting on the snow by himself, just staring motionless at that light. Somehow I'm relieved, and the sight of him like that stays with me. The aurora spreads in stages until it covers the entire sky, a stream of shooting stars falling through it.

K the boy general is busy feeding firewood to the cabin stove. I can't tell whether he has seen enough of the northern lights or doesn't intend to look at them at all. But perhaps what the kids are feeling now is not important. The memories of children are not something that we can fathom. As far as I'm concerned, they can forget all about Ruth Glacier when they return to their busy routines in Japan. What I want to know is how it has sat with them in five or ten years. Because a single experience often needs time to mature and take shape inside a person.

The Ruth Glacier is a barren alpine world of nothing but rock, ice, snow and stars, the complete reverse of the ocean of every kind of information in which the children of Japan abide. But in exchange for all that it lacks, this place has the silent presence of the cosmos. The quiet of a night spent atop a glacier, the cold of the wind, the sparkle of the stars . . . Scarcity of information holds within it a certain power, endowing us with an opportunity to imagine something.

Scenes observed in childhood can linger in the mind forever. When we become adults and stand at the various crossroads of life, often it isn't the words of people that give us courage and heart but a landscape seen long ago.

The day we descend from the mountains, we are bathed in early-spring light and see Denali shining white in the distance.

Another Kind of Time

I had a memorable conversation with a friend one time while we were camped out on a glacier beneath a night sky so clear it was almost raining stars. We were waiting for the aurora, and even when it showed no signs of appearing we remained sitting in the snow, gazing at the cosmos. An astounding number of lights twinkled in the moonless void, the occasional shooting star drawing a trail as it flew by.

'Wouldn't it be amazing if you could see all these stars every night in a huge city like Tokyo... You'd glance up on your way home after a hard day's work and find the universe right there, almost within arm's reach. I don't care what kind of person you are. At the end of the day there'd be something going through your head.'

'One time someone asked me this. Imagine you're all alone looking at a sky full of stars like this one, or at a sunset that could almost bring you to tears. If there was a person you loved out there somewhere, how would you convey that beauty and your feeling at that moment to them?'

'I guess I'd take a picture. Or if I was good at painting, I'd paint it on a canvas. Or forget that – maybe I'd just tell them about it in words.'

'The person that asked me this question said, "I'd show them by changing . . . By the way the powerful feeling I got looking at the sunset changed me."'

Throughout the various stages of our lives, nature sends us a multiplicity of messages. Whether you're a child new to this world or an elder about to pass away, the story it tells each of us is different.

I can still recall even now the beauty of twilight when I was a young child, as I ran home for dinner after watching a *kamishibai* performance in the field near our home. I wonder sometimes how I perceived my surroundings and the passage of time back then. Amid the sadness of the day coming to its end, did I arrive at some vague realization even at that age that I too would not exist forever? Perhaps such understanding is a child's first instinctive way of relating to the world. If I look back on my own childhood, I can think of several events that allowed me to see nature from a fresh perspective, each of which was like a small crossroads that I encountered as I made my way finally to Alaska.

The first was a movie I happened to see at the local theater when I was in elementary school. The title was *Tiko and the Shark*. Set on Tahiti as development of the tourism industry was transforming the face of the island, it is the tale of an understated romance between a young girl on a sightseeing visit from Europe and an indigenous boy named Chico who befriends a shark. What especially captivated me about the film was the blue expanse of the southern Pacific Ocean stretching endlessly in the background. I remember that the pamphlet I bought at the entrance described it as the first nature film shot on location without any Hollywood sets. At the time, I had been watching nothing but samurai sword-fighting flicks and this sudden exposure to the vastness of the world must have made an enormous impact on me; to this day I can still recall the name of the girl: Diana.

As a teenager, I became deeply fascinated with the wilderness of Hokkaido, which seemed so remote and distant from the Tokyo suburb where I grew up. My interest extended to the brown bears native to that region and although I was reading all sorts of books, it was these great beasts, relatives of the grizzly, that began to occupy my mind. I could be on a juddering train or among the jostling crowds of the metropolis, when my thoughts would turn to them without warning, and it would strike me as unaccountably strange that brown bears were out there, in the same country as me, living and breathing at that very moment. While I was going about my routine in the city, one of them was bound to be climbing over a fallen tree as it lumbered its way through a mountain forest . . . There should have been nothing surprising about such obvious facts and yet they lingered with me in my adolescence, kindling my curiosity about nature and the universe. Although I didn't know how to express my sense of wonder at that age, I now view it as my first inkling of the way in which the same time flows equally for all things. Perhaps it even represents the first instance that

I became conscious of the world, in my own callow way, not as a piece of knowledge but through intuition.

Several years ago, a friend of mine expressed a similar idea. An incessantly busy Tokyo editor, she just barely managed to arrange the week off to fly over and accompany me on an expedition to photograph whales. She had worked until late just the previous night, so the Southeast summer sea was for her like a whole new reality, magically appearing as though she had turned the page of a book.

One day at dusk, we came across a school of humpback whales and followed behind them slowly in our little boat while they swam along blowing spray into the air. When we were close enough to feel their exhalations on our faces, we found ourselves part of an overwhelming scene, with glaciers and primeval forest all around, and the nature of everything breathing in harmony amid the everlasting flow of time. My friend leaned on the gunwale with a pleasant breeze on her skin, transfixed by these leviathans crashing ahead.

Then all of a sudden a whale leaped from the surface of the water right in front of us. As though in slow motion, its enormous body launched up whirling into the air, hung there for the briefest moment and then fell gradually back down, sending up an explosive splash.

Calm returned eventually to the sea and the school began to roll onwards as though nothing had happened. I had seen breaching on several occasions, but never had I witnessed it at such close proximity. I doubt human beings will ever understand what it is that whales are trying to convey in this act, even as we seek interpretations for all animal behavior.

Maybe they just want to feel the breeze or simply jump for the heck of it.

In any case, my friend was rendered speechless by what had just unfolded. I think that what struck her about the spectacle was not so much the enormous whale itself but the encompassing expanses of nature that framed it – that is, the smallness of the whale and the time they shared together, even if it was only an instant. Here is how she described the experience a long while afterwards.

I had so much work to do, but I'm really glad I went. What did I like about it? I guess it was the realization that any time I'm slaving away in Tokyo, a whale could be leaping from the sea somewhere in Alaska . . . After I got back, I thought over what I was going to tell everyone about the trip, but I didn't know what to say. In the end, I just couldn't find the words.

Flowing gently and determinately outside the moments of our mundane routines is another kind of time. Hold onto awareness of this truth in some corner of your mind throughout the daily grind and gain a great power for living.

In Search of Totem Poles

The original ancestors of the indigenous peoples of the Americas are believed to have crossed from northern Asia to what is now Alaska along the Bering land bridge that once connected North America and Eurasia. This was approximately eighteen thousand years ago, just as the last Ice Age was finally drawing to a close. Caught up in everlasting currents of time, many of these early migrants gradually spread south through an unknown continent, while some settled on the coast of what is now southeastern Alaska. This latter group formed two tribes, the Tlingit and the Haida, who are the progenitors of the totem pole.

The mysterious figures carved into totem poles – bald eagles, ravens, whales, grizzlies – serve as palpable memories of the distant forebears and traditions of these peoples. Yet they are not monuments built to last, as the cultures they record were based not around stone but the evanescent medium of wood.

So what if there was some way in the modern era, on the verge of the twenty-first century, to see an old totem pole left to slumber in the woods somewhere? Not a new totem pole made for tourists or one of those artifacts arrayed in museums, but a real-live totem pole that had maintained continuity with the age of myth. I didn't care if it had collapsed onto the forest floor or decayed into mulch, I wanted to touch one with my bare hands. It was while I was traveling through the wilderness of Alaska in recent years that this desire began to crystalize in my mind.

I started to ask around for leads but everyone just laughed at me. I remember one time in particular when I inquired with a group of Southeast loggers.

'Have you ever seen an old totem pole in a forest?' I asked. 'Even a rotten one?'

'No way you're going to find one of those things around,' one of the men replied. 'Not in this day and age. You'd have to have been born a hundred years ago.'

You can certainly find decorative totem poles erected in some indigenous towns. But even if they have retained the same form, the mythic beings depicted – like Whale and Eagle and Bear – have departed to somewhere far beyond our reach with the dramatic change these communities have undergone. And with the disappearance of the old stories from the minds of those who carve them, the poles no longer have anything to impart.

Then just last summer, a surprising piece of news reached my ears: there were still totem poles on the Queen Charlotte Islands!

Located in northern British Columbia, just south of the Canadian border with Alaska, this remote archipelago was home to six thousand Haida when the Europeans arrived in the nineteenth century, bringing smallpox that wiped out seventy per cent of the population and triggered an exodus of those that remained. In the twentieth century, the museums of the Great Powers set about collecting artifacts from around the world and the abandoned villages of Queen Charlotte were no exception. As numerous totem poles were being hauled away, descendants of the Haida survivors banded together in protest, fighting to allow their sacred spaces to decay in peace and adamantly resisting external pressures that sought preservation of the totem poles in the name of their historical value. The upshot of all this is that one Haida village has been left untouched for a hundred years.

The sea around the Queen Charlotte Islands is rough today and tosses my inflatable raft about like the leaf of a tree in the wind. Deep forest spills out to the shore of all the archipelago's numerous islands, unchanged from the age in which people lived side by side with totem poles. It is as though I am traveling into the past, a feeling enhanced somehow by the dreary weather, as mist ripples from tree to tree like some shapeshifting creature and the leaden sky pours.

Up ahead, breakers crash on a line of rocks along the shore, where I spot a small easy-to-overlook gap that leads to an inlet. When my motor gets tangled in a patch of thick algae, I turn it off and paddle the rest of the way. Then, passing between boulders that rise on both sides like a gate, I enter the sheltered waters beyond and am immediately greeted by unbelievable quiet.

At the back of a tiny strip of beach is a row of what looks like huge naked trees, different from those filling the dense woods surrounding them. Here at last are the long-weathered totem poles I have yearned to see, standing on this silent beach that still harbors the dreams and joys and sorrows and anger of a people through the passage of time.

The faint roar of the Pacific rises to my ears again, and with one last stroke of the paddle I lift the boat onto a small wave that carries it up onto the sand. The rain has settled to a light sprinkle when I disembark and climb from the beach onto the adjacent bank, almost overwhelmed with excitement as I approach.

The totem poles I find are covered with moss and plants that have made them their homes. Most are already tilted and several lie toppled on the ground. Even so, their faded carvings seem rich with meaning. A human child cradled in the arms of a bear, a frog's face peeking from between the fins of a whale, a bald eagle on top as though watching over the village . . .

Eventually I step over to the foot of one and gaze up at it for a time. A huge tree rises from the top of the looming shaft, with roots that reach down its length to the ground. I can tell from the shape of the upper section that this totem pole is a tomb, as I have learned about the Haida practice of hollowing out one end for burial purposes. The seed of a spruce that happened to fall in one day must have used the nutrients of the human body to take root, before feeding on the totem pole the way some saplings feed on dead trunks, as it grew and grew over the months and years.

When I brush my way through a patch of tall grass, a further surprise awaits me. Amid the early-spring green crouches a newborn white-tailed deer. After I have waited at a distance for a while, its mother emerges from the trees and they begin to move between the totem poles, munching on grass as they go. Soon the doe and her fawn enter a deep grassy hollow of about a hundred square feet over which four mossy logs lean like a roof, where they continue to graze placidly. I am transfixed by the spectacle; they are in the ruins of what was once a Haida habitation. Humans vacated the site and now nature is slowly but surely taking it back. This firsthand understanding of what has become of the place dawns on me with an emotional force that is not so much saddening as humbling.

Presently the rain ceases and the sun begins to shine through the trees. I sit on the rocks by the shore, as the sea sparkles in the gloaming. I am resting my body on an exceedingly comfortable boulder with a groove for my back when a vision comes to me that seems certain to be true: one time long long ago, someone sat on this very boulder and gazed upon this ocean at twilight just like I am at this moment.

A woman cradles a sobbing baby, soothing it as she walks. Men returned from fishing drag their canoe up onto the sand. Young boys and girls frolic as they approach these rocks . . . Such scenes arise and dissipate one after the other in my mind's eye.

Evidence of human settlement on this island is said to go back seven thousand years, whereas the last totem poles that existed in the age of myth will no doubt vanish without a trace into the forest within a mere fifty. The myriad dreamlike folktales that their carvings represent blur the lines between stories about humans and stories about animals, suggesting a kind of wisdom accumulated by their makers instinctively in their interactions with nature to help them survive across time. They are, moreover, a kind of power that we have lost.

History races inexorably through a fog with no goal in sight. If humanity wishes to continue to exist in the future, the day may come when we will have to create our own myths once again and stake our lives on them.

Tap, tap, tap. The sound of something striking wood startles me from my reverie and I look around for its source, but see no one. Then, glancing upwards, I spot a woodpecker that has alighted on a totem pole and is pecking away at the timeworn face of a grizzly. At some point another deer emerges from the forest and begins to meander between the poles. Before I know it, the myths have been reborn and the moss-covered face of Raven, creator of this world, is staring down upon me with unwavering eyes.

My First Encounter
with Alaska

One day I receive a call from Don Ross.

'There's a photographer from *National Geographic* in town,' he says. 'Sounds like he's about to head to the Arctic to shoot the caribou migration. Wants to pick your brain about it. Would you mind going to meet him at his hotel? Name is George Mobley.'

National Geographic. The most prestigious magazine in America when it comes to history, nature, geography, culture. Landing your work in that fine rag has got to be every photographer's dream. Now here's one of their staff photographers. I bet he's rushing around the globe.

Such are the thoughts swirling in my head as I drive downtown to the hotel, when the name George Mobley suddenly rings a bell.

It can't be . . . But I'm almost certain that was his name.

Doing a U-turn, I return home and take down a book of photographs from my shelf. It doesn't take a moment to find the page. On it is a picture that calls up old memories and, sure enough, written to the side in small print is 'George Mobley'. Who would have thought that I would meet him like this?

In my adolescence, I read all sorts of books and through them developed a fascination with the wilderness of Hokkaido, which seemed to me at that age like some unimaginably distant land. Eventually my interest in northern regions shifted to even more distant Alaska, but with no way for me to discover what it was really like there my curiosity just went on growing unchecked. In the Japan of the late 1960s, even books on Alaska were almost impossible to come by.

Then one day, I was in the Kanda secondhand bookshop area, browsing at a store that specialized in Western books, when I came across a collection of photographs of Alaska. With all the other foreign titles lined up on the shelf, who can say why my gaze stopped on that particular book? But there it was, right in front of me, as though awaiting my arrival all along. And from then on, wherever I went, whether to school or anywhere else, it was always in my bag. There's an old saying for this: 'Read a book over till your fingers stain it.' Of course in my case, it wasn't the words but the photographs that absorbed me.

One image called to me with such force that I couldn't help but turn to its page every time I picked up the book. It was an aerial shot of an Inuit village in the Arctic Circle. The grey waters of the Bering Sea, the sinking leaden sky, the bamboo reeds of sunlight shining down through breaks in the clouds . . . And, smack dab in the middle of this, a lone dot of human habitation.

The scene was utterly desolate, and I think what first struck me about it was the uncanniness of the light. But over time it was the village that began to capture my attention. Although I could make out the shape of the buildings, no figures were visible among them, and I wondered what had compelled people to live in such a place, practically at the ends of the Earth. Who were they? What sort of thoughts ran through their heads from day to day?

Sometimes when I was younger, while gazing absentmindedly from a train over a city at twilight, I would spot through the window of someone's home a family gathered in happy conversation, possibly having dinner. Always I would keep my eyes fixed on this diorama until the glow of the window passed out of sight. Then my chest would tighten with some surging emotion that I'm not sure what to call. Wonder at these strangers living lives unknown to me? Sadness at existing in the same era without ever having the chance to become acquainted?

This feeling was similar to the one that arose when I looked at the picture. The difference in the case of the villagers, however, was that I wanted more than anything to meet them.

The caption on the photograph was the name of the village: Shishmaref. I decided I would try sending a letter. But to whom exactly? And to what address? Opening a Japanese–English dictionary, I found the word 'mayor'. For the address, my only option was to add 'Alaska' and 'America' to the village's name.

'I saw a picture of your town in a book. I would like to visit. I will help out in any way I can but is there anyone who I could stay with?'

That was the gist of it, an honest expression of exactly what I was thinking. I can only speculate now how clumsy the wording was; it was the first time I had ever written a letter in English.

Time passed and no reply was forthcoming. Not that this surprised me. I hadn't even included a definite address or recipient. And imagine if the letter did reach one of the villagers. Who was going to host someone they had never even met?

I soon completely forgot that I had even sent it. Until one day, six months later, I returned home from school to find that an envelope had arrived from overseas. A letter from a family in Shishmaref.

We got your letter. I talked with my wife about you coming to our house . . . Summer is the season of the reindeer hunt. We need people to help out . . . Come anytime.

Six months later, I was on my way to Alaska. After transferring between several small airplanes, the village finally came into view, surrounded by the Bering Sea. Reality merged with the image I had obsessed over and I kept my face pressed to the glass, overcome by the moment.

My sojourn in Shishmaref those three summer months at the age of nineteen stayed with me ever after. To actually set foot in the village I had viewed from above in the photograph;

to hunt bears, seals and reindeer for the first time; to meet all the villagers beneath the midnight sun . . . Intense experiences came one after the next, sedimenting in the depths of my soul and leaving me with an abiding interest in the diversity of ways of life.

I decided afterwards that I would pursue photography as a profession and returned to Alaska seven years later, bearing many dreams in my heart. This time my visit would not be so brief. I was expecting to stay three, no, maybe five years, but the arrow of time just flew by. I trekked the pristine slopes and valleys of the Brooks Range that spans the polar regions of the state. I listened to the grinding of great mountains of ice as I voyaged by kayak through Glacier Bay. I paddled an *umiak* after right whales in the Arctic Ocean. I followed herds of caribou, enchanted by their migration. I recorded a year in the life of a bear. Gazed up at countless northern lights. Crossed paths with wolves. Immersed myself in the cultures of many peoples . . . Before I knew it, ten years had passed. Somewhere along the way I had put aside thoughts of leaving and found myself building a house as I tried to put down roots in this land.

So was picking up that particular book at that specific time in that one bookstore the predestined event that was responsible for my coming to Alaska? The answer, I think, is no. For if you attempt to trace back each moment in your life, all you'll find is a chain of innumerable coincidences stretching off without end like your reflections in two opposing mirrors.

Nevertheless, I did in fact go to the town of Shishmaref after seeing that picture. And there's no denying that a shift took place in my life, as though a new map had been drawn for me. All of which brings me back to the man who took the picture, George Mobley.

When I arrive at the hotel, I find my way to his room and knock at the door. Unaware of how much this meeting means to me, George comes to greet me, a smile beaming from his white-bearded face.

After we've talked caribou for a while, I take out the old book and begin to tell him the whole story. I'm glad to find his eyes focused intently on mine as he listens.

'Wow . . . So my picture changed your whole life . . .'

'Not exactly . . . More like it opened up a big opportunity for me.'

'And do you regret it?' Just beginning to advance in years, George smiles softly in the depths of his eyes.

Life abounds with hidden springs and levers that influence the direction we take, as we pass by countless others from day to day without ever meeting. Yet the primordial sadness this brings is also what leads to the fathomless mystery of our coming together.

Lituya Bay

As the Cessna lifts off from the village of Yakutat in southern Alaska and begins to carry us straight east along the coast, I look out the window at the bleak and rugged shoreline. Formed of glaciers spilling into the Pacific from the lofty mountains of the Fairweather Range, it stretches on and on for some hundred and fifty miles.

Every time we fly over a glacier, the pilot lowers our altitude, and I press my face to the glass, gazing in awe at the icy terrain spread out below. I can see the places where the edges of glaciers have scraped away at woodland, exposing earth and scattering countless ice floes and trees across the area. Patches of pitch-black ground hosting plant life might be mistaken for land if not for faint whitish-blue fault lines that reveal the frozen mass underneath. The scene is more chaotic than beautiful, offering a vivid reminder that the Ice Age was not so long ago as we often imagine.

I am on my way to Lituya Bay, a secluded inlet that I have been wanting to visit for some time due to my fascination with the life of a hermit who once lived there. He wasn't a man who had done anything of major historical importance, but he was the only white person ever to settle on this inhospitable stretch of coastline – and from a certain perspective that was itself kind of historic.

Although my interest in the history of Alaska goes back many years, it only deepened after I moved here and found myself insatiably curious about certain questions. What was it that brought people to Alaska? What path did they choose to take in the years that followed? Historical epochs come and go, but the sort of challenges we each face in our lifetimes do not vary nearly as much. Something about the life of that hermit must have resonated in some way with my own.

His name was Jim Huscroft. As far as I can determine, he rowed a boat up to a small island in Lituya Bay sometime between 1915 and 1917 and lived there by himself for the twenty-two years that remained to him. This description in the Alaskan classic *Glacier Bay: The Land and the Silence*, though short, made a big impression on me. The book also records the following account, from renowned mountaineer and cartographer Bradford Washburn, of what a great person Huscroft was:

Jim Huscroft was one of the kindest men I have ever known. When I first met him in 1932, he was living alone on Cenotaph Island in Lituya Bay, where he had lived for some seventeen years as a sort of modern hermit, going 'out' to Juneau once a year to buy supplies and to sell furs of the blue foxes that ran wild on the island.

Aside from what small income the foxes earned him, Jim was completely self-sufficient. The only photograph of him included in the book has him smiling shyly while he holds a bunch of potatoes pulled from his garden. It was this smile that called to me somehow. The account of Jim continues:

When Jim took his small boat to Juneau on his annual trip to the outside, he always went first to a store where he could buy a tub of salt mackerel. He ate one or two on the spot and then put away the rest of the tub to take to the island.

Jim also went to the Elks Club to pick up a year's worth of newspapers that he had had put aside for him. Then he would return to the island and would read each morning the newspaper from exactly a year ago. He swore that he never cheated by reading ahead.

When a stranger arrived at Cenotaph Island, whether by boat or float plane, Jim was always there to greet him. His bald head gleaming dully, he would be waiting, watch in hand, with the words, 'I make it eleven twenty: what do you make it?'

He helped anyone who came to the island and offered them what hospitality he could. The following conversation reportedly occurred after Jim read an article about poor children in New York and is a perfect illustration of how essentially human he was.

> 'Say it ain't so, Bob. Say it ain't so.' I said, 'What ain't so, Jim?' and he replied, 'That the kids in New York City is eatin' out of garbage pails! I've been thinkin' about it all winter . . . There's all those salmon in the Bay and goats in the hills an' if I could just get some cans I could help some. Tain't right for kids to be eatin' that way, you know, an' I want to help 'em out. Been thinking about it all winter.'

Jim's humanity is at the same time an example of the diverse ways of being that the human organism can realize.

> The great climax of each year for Jim Huscroft was Christmas dinner. He planned the momentous affair months ahead, and always showed us strawberries and blueberries and salmonberries he had put up, to be used when the time came for Christmas baking. When the exciting occasion arrived Jim would sit down, entirely alone, to a roast-goose dinner with a choice of fourteen different kinds of pie.

Apart from the fact that Jim was born in the state of Ohio and that he earned large fortunes at three separate times only to lose them on failed ventures, nothing is known about what he did before arriving in Alaska. He passed away on March 23rd,

1939. The following year, Washburn carved his epitaph and buried it among the rocks of the island.

That's all there is to tell about Jim Huscroft, but for whatever reason his story stuck with me. And his death would not mark the end of the chronicle of Lituya Bay, which would link eventually to a legend of the Tlingit people that formerly inhabited the region.

It was once said that in the mouth of the bay, at the bottom of the sea, there lurked a demon called Kah Lituya. All who approached his waters he brought to ruin, transforming them into bears who must watch over the bay from the mountaintops as his slaves. If anyone dared to enter the bay, he would drop boulders from the slopes and raise a huge wave to swallow these intruders into the depths.

By Jim's time, the Tlingit people had vanished from the land, outlived by their legend. Yet they knew the truth: Kah Lituya had shown his face long long ago and was destined to one day return again . . .

July 9th, 1958. The skies are clear and the ocean still, as a party of eight Canadian climbers camp out near the mouth of Lituya Bay, having completed their ascent of Mount Fairweather.

8pm. A trawler, the *Edrie*, returns to the bay and sets down anchor.

9pm. A small airplane lands on the beach to pick up the climbers, then takes off for Juneau. (The original plan, reportedly, was for it to arrive the following morning.) Some minutes later, two more fishing boats – the *Badger* and the *Sunmore* enter.

10:16pm. The sun is down and the tide is out when Mount Fairweather moves.

Triggered by a fierce earthquake, ninety million tons of rock fall, a glacier crumbles and an enormous tsunami rising some hundred and thirty feet rips through Lituya Bay at a speed of a hundred miles per hour. The *Sunmore* is instantly sucked under the sea while the *Badger* and the *Edrie* are carried above the treetops to a height of sixty-five feet. Researchers from the American Geographical Society who arrive the following morning will later describe the scene as apocalyptic. And washed away forever by the wave are the old cabin and vegetable patch of Jim Huscroft.

Through gaps in the clouds, I can now see Lituya Bay and the ice-covered ridges of the Fairweather Range. In spite of the name, this stretch of coastline is known to have the worst weather in all of Alaska; it is rare for the sky to be so clear.

Soon the plane banks around behind the slopes, revealing the entirety of the bay below us. Then we make our descent and land on the narrow strip of beach.

Once the engines are off, all I can hear are the waves of the Pacific. I spot the faint paw prints of a bear in the sand. Following the tracks to a rocky ledge with a clear vantage, I look out over the length and breadth of Cenotaph Island, the place that Jim once called home. Glacier-hugging mountains loom over fifteen thousand feet before me. It is a breathtaking scene. Can paradise and danger exist side by side?

I am here to see the landscape that Jim looked upon for twenty-two years. While he and I may have been born in different eras, we both came to Alaska in search of something. I want to touch his life. That's all this journey is for.

There is no longer any way to find out why he decided to settle here. Everyone has their own unique story and path that they must follow. But there's one thing I am almost sure of. The day that Jim Huscroft paddled his little boat through the mouth of the inlet, out here at the very edge of the world, the sky over Lituya Bay must have been clear and the air infinitely calm, just like today.

Kiska

The rolling waves of the Bering Sea roused me from a dream. I was on an American Navy vessel passing through the Aleutian Islands on its way to Kiska. It was now morning and the mild storm that struck around midnight seemed to have finally moved on.

When I went up on deck, I could already see Kiska approaching. Like the other islands in the Aleutian chain, its shores are completely devoid of trees, no doubt due to the powerful winds that blast them relentlessly. The waters in this region are known to be rough, plagued as they are by low-pressure systems, and one official document goes so far as to call them 'the worst on Earth'. But although the highlands were shrouded in mist that morning, the weather was unusually mild, with beams of sunlight breaking intermittently through the clouds.

Gazing at the island was Toyotaro Sugano, a seventy-one-year-old veteran of the Pacific War. Originally from Yamagata Prefecture, Sugano was on a garrison that succeeded in a miraculous evacuation of Kiska on July 29th, 1943. It was two months earlier that two thousand six hundred and thirty-eight of his compatriots on Attu Island had become so-called *gyokusai*, 'shattered jewels' that threw away their lives in an infamous suicide assault on their American combatants.

'Nice to see the sun out,' I said.

'For fifty years now I've been dreaming of setting foot on Kiska again,' said Sugano. His face, darkly tanned from years of farming, broke into a smile. 'This is the day that has kept me going. My wishes must have been heard.'

While we were talking, George Earle had appeared on deck, a veteran of the same war but for the opposing side. Now almost eighty years old, he was one of the six and a half thousand American soldiers who, unaware of the evacuation, landed eighteen days later to retake the then deserted Kiska. As a member of the mountain infantry, George was on the vanguard of what turned out to be a needlessly tense amphibious assault. Now half a century later, Sugano and George were joining a group of veterans, including one other Japanese and nine other Americans, to visit the island for the first time since World War II.

Somewhat bashfully, Sugano bowed low to George with a morning greeting in Japanese; and George responded in English with a 'good morning' and a slight wave. As the green slopes of Kiska filled my vision, I thought about the long stretch of time that had separated these two men from this moment.

They may have been unable to communicate in words, but next thing I noticed they had their arms around each other's shoulders.

The Pacific War can seem far removed to those of us who were born after it ended. Lacking direct experience of the era, we can conceive it only as information in the pages of history, and try as we might to approach the reality of the past, our knowledge will never compare to having actually been there. For Japan it was an imperialistic war of obsessive territorial expansion, while for America it was one military theater in a fight against fascism. Yet studying these narratives after the fact yields no true understanding of why three million one hundred thousand lives on the Japanese side alone had to be thrown away, as all of us are inevitably bound to the age in which we are born.

Even such bewildering body counts fall short of conveying to us the horror of war. Our only hope of comprehending it would be to somehow experience for ourselves the irreplaceable life of each unnamed individual numbered among the dead and what remained of the lives of those they left behind. This point struck me poignantly several years ago after I finished reading Hisae Sawachi's *O Ocean, Sleep Thee Well: The Living and the Dead of Midway*, a non-fiction tome that provides detailed accounts of the tragic lives of over three thousand Japanese and American youths who were sucked from near and far into that vortex called the Battle of Midway, as well as the accounts of their surviving parents, sweethearts and wives in the aftermath. Serving as a record of the inherent absurdity that makes war resistant to any adequate definition, the book contains a particularly moving quote from the widow of one American soldier:

> Now I understand why we long for days gone by and build up faith in the continued existence of the dead. Our hearts cannot accept that an individual life, a person who we deeply loved and completely depended on, is gone forever. We simply refuse to come to terms with it.

Japan's invasion of the Aleutians, along with its occupation of Kiska and Attu, is thought to have been a diversion from the crucial sea battle at Midway Atoll. Once Japanese forces had lost there, a turning point in the Pacific War, the island chain no longer had strategic value and was soon abandoned. The *gyokusai* charge in Attu was the first of its kind and soon triggered a wave of these desperate maneuvers in Japan's rush towards defeat. On Kiska, by contrast, a garrison of five and a half thousand soldiers used the archipelago's copious fog as cover to evacuate the island in a mere forty minutes.

Four days prior to this remarkable escape, an American fighter plane had been shot down on the island. When a group of Japanese soldiers rushed over to the crash site, the young second lieutenant inside was already dead. In honor of his valor, the fifty men present put up a cross to mark his grave and inscribed a plaque with the English words: 'Sleeping here a brave hero who lost youth and happiness for his Motherland!'

In an age in which one government slogan was 'Demon Brutes Those Yanks and Brits!' this show of respect was not something the soldiers could have ever risked admitting to anyone else. According to Sugano, who helped put up the post, he brought his palms together and called out to the deceased: 'Soon enough, we too will die. Let us share stories in the world to come.'

An American lieutenant who remembered the grave post after the war was the central organizer for this joint Japanese-American memorial service on Kiska. While some participants may have once been enemies, what united them all were memories of their time in this island's harsh environment.

I am grateful for the opportunity I had to spend five days with these dozen veterans, averaging nearly eighty years of age. I walked in the mountains with them, listening to remembrances of their service here and visiting various war ruins. We saw rusted antiaircraft cannons scattered across the tundra, cruisers run aground on a sandy beach, and even Special Attack Unit midget submarines – those two-seater suicide crafts of the deep – loaded with torpedoes and only enough fuel to reach their target.

'One of the Americans told me something today,' Sugano muttered wistfully at night in his tent. 'He said that we Japanese are too reckless with our lives, that we need to treat ourselves with greater dignity . . .'

I could tell that Sugano had thoughts of his wartime days that he wanted to express but was struggling to find the words.

One day, after gathering the August flowers of Kiska, a brief memorial was held at which Sugano gave a eulogy, his voice cracking many times as he wiped away his tears.

'Hoshino-san, I fulfilled my duty,' he told me afterwards, squeezing my hand between both of his. What could someone like me, who has never known war, have possibly said in response? It was on that day that Sugano finally stepped out of the shadow of the war.

On another day, we were greeted with uncommonly clear Aleutian weather, which each member took advantage of in their own way. In a patch of tall grass beside a sheer cliff, I found George setting up his canvas alone. He told me how he always liked to paint and used to teach art at the college in his hometown after the war. I sat in the grass nearby and soaked up the end-of-summer sunlight. Kiska Bay was sparkling and war seemed like a dream.

'What sort of position do the days after the war occupy in your life?' I asked.

George's paintbrush went still and he stared at the Bering Sea, thinking for a while.

'The weight that war left on my shoulders is too heavy to fathom. We were so young. Our lives were just about to begin. When my wife died right after the war, I bottled up all my memories of it. I only started turning up at the reunions of other mountain infantry four, five years ago. What must have finally opened me up was remarrying and putting together a new life . . .'

A bald eagle wheeled about leisurely on rising currents of air. This isolated island is one of the world's more important seabird roosts. I recalled a story that George had brought up at one point about a friend of his from the war, who was infatuated with birds. The man was so taken with watching them while stationed on Kiska that they struck him off the roll. Apparently, the moment the war ended, he returned to the island as a researcher for the Smithsonian Institute. Political systems and social structures inevitably change from one era to the next. Only ways of life and the dreams of individuals steadfastly persist.

On the night before we left Kiska, George came over to tell me something.

'Michio, about what I said on the cliff earlier – there's one thing I forgot to mention. I liked to paint Kiska in those days. It captivated me. But somehow I completely missed the smaller wilderness beneath my feet. The tiny flowers of the tundra, the grass blowing in the breeze and the beauty of the moss . . . I come back here fifty years later and now I finally notice. That's all I wanted to tell you.'

Death of a Bush Pilot

We've been having a wonderful autumn in Fairbanks this year. I wasn't expecting to be feeling so sad as the season approaches its end. Although several bush pilots I know have lost their lives in the past couple of years, I don't think anyone could have guessed that this one would be next.

Roger Dowding has died in a plane crash.

'It's the end of an era.' This is the refrain on the lips of many of my friends and colleagues in their inconsolable grief. There could no more objective way to describe Roger's death. Yes, an era has truly come to an end.

None of this is to imply that Roger was some Arctic bush-pilot extraordinaire, some hotshot famed for his record of legendary flights, or anything of that nature. On the contrary, such portraits of glory in the cockpit do not at all fit the man that Roger was.

A shy but sociable person, Roger had a sense of humor that emerged slowly. When he laughed, crinkles would form beside the eyes set in his squarish face, displaying a profound kind of sadness from the depth of his mirthful expression. He also had a peculiar power to warm people's hearts of which he was completely oblivious himself. All of us love the man that he was as he exists in each of our personal recollections.

When on August 29th all communication with Roger was lost during a blizzard over the Brooks Range, I couldn't stop thinking about our mutual friend Don Ross. As fellow bush pilots who had flown the skies of Arctic Alaska together for years, the two men were bound in friendship deep and true. Seeing them in each other's company always brought me joy.

When Roger's whereabouts still remained unknown, many of his bush-pilot friends gathered in the indigenous community of Arctic Village to search for him. But with first snow already covering the mountains, there was little hope of spotting his white Cessna. It was Don alone who persisted in flying to the last, tempting a second accident when the weather took a turn for the worse. He even traced Roger's flight path on foot through the early-winter Brooks Range. And just when everyone else was about to call the search off, saying it would be impossible until spring, Don found in the upper Sheenjek Valley his beloved friend's forlorn white fuselage.

Under clear skies on a Sunday in September, a memorial service is now being held. A hangar for small airplanes on the edge of the airport has been chosen as the venue. It brims with memories for everyone as this is where Roger always serviced his Cessna. Filling the basketball-court-sized space is an ample spread of foods and some two hundred of Roger's friends. The decorations consist of his photo albums and of letters from those who couldn't make it. It is a memorial in the true spirit of both Alaska and Roger, with everyone dressed casually and several large dogs roaming about.

To the wall Don sticks a large sheet of paper on which is written in magic marker, 'Thank you for not puking.' These words used to hang in the shack Roger called his office, expressing jocular appreciation to his passengers for putting up with the rough ride. Don's desire to send off Roger's soul in an atmosphere of cheer is palpable. I can't bear to face him. I'm liable to burst into tears.

The hangar is crowded with people I haven't seen in ages, their faces puffy from crying. One of them is my friend Kim Heacox. He is the author of *Bush Pilots of Alaska,* a photobook that contains a memorable anecdote about Roger. When Kim is trying to convince his aspiring pilot of a nephew to become an Alaskan bush pilot rather than pursue a career at a major airline, he tells the young man a story. It concerns a retired airlines captain who takes a recreational flight to the Sheenjek River on Roger's Cessna 185.

The pilot flew low over the river and studied a wind sock in an alder next to a short gravel bar. He made another flyover and said, 'She looks good.' Everyone held on for a white-knuckle landing. The Cessna skimmed a bluff, kissed the gravel bar, rumbled towards the river and swung around with five feet to spare. The retired captain was flabbergasted. That afternoon he sat atop a hill and quietly watched the bush pilot bring the 185 in and out, ferrying gear, landing and taking off repeatedly without a hitch. As he watched the final flawless landing and takeoff he said, 'You know, for thirty years all I really did was sit in the cockpit of a Boeing jet and run a computer. But this guy, he's a real pilot.'

The memorial officially begins an hour past schedule. A packed circle forms as people keep pouring in. The proceedings are facilitated by Don and the Brooks Range guide Jim Jones. Don kicks everything off by drawing a scrap of paper from his pocket to read a poem.

'Here's a man who fancies himself a bush pilot writing poetry,' says Jim as he introduces Don. 'A weirdo if there ever was one.'

The crowd erupts with laughter. Jim, another empathetic man, has intuited the audience well.

Don's poem is made up of memories from his flights with Roger over the Arctic. The odyssey of the caribou repeated since time unknown. The tiny flowers that bloom in the summer tundra. The wind that sweeps through. The finitude of all life. We listen rapt to Don's deep hushed voice, moved by his simple words.

Next is Jim's turn to read a poem. It is titled 'The Man Who Loved Spam'. The epithet is true. Roger was partial to the canned ham, that American emblem of the worst food imaginable. The hangar explodes with laughter. And everyone cries as they laugh.

The bereaved subsequently begin to share memories of Roger. There is no set order; one person picks up organically where another leaves off. I feel obliged to say my part but ultimately hold the memory inside. It was the day of a spring photoshoot I flew to with Roger. I wish I could recall how many years ago.

Having passed over the early-spring valleys of the Brooks Range, we were on our way to the Arctic Ocean to view the seasonal migration of the caribou. That year, Roger had bought his first video camera, a small device, and was panning it about the whole ride from Fairbanks. Bouncing off the walls like a little child, he kept aiming the lens at me and having me say something. I still have that tape in my possession.

Soon we were approaching the Kongakut River, along which I planned to set up camp, but due to an early thaw that year we couldn't find a place to land anywhere. The memory of what happened next remains seared in my mind. Roger went in for countless test landings on the overflow ice (formed when water rising between cracks in the river ice freezes in a second layer). He would skim his skis over the ice, feeling out its condition as he glided along the surface, before whirling up to repeat the process.

'I have never made such a dangerous landing,' Roger confessed to me much later. When he finally went in for the actual landing, we could hear the sound of ice cracking as the Cessna drew safely to a stop, sweat-drenched in the sub-zero air.

The memorial is winding down. Small balloons are handed out so that we can all send our thoughts to Roger. Once the enormous door of the hanger has been raised, the sky spreads crystal blue outside. Cool air soothes my tear-spent face. A Cessna lifts off from the ground right then, rising into the fall sky.

The idea is to release the balloons into the air while Roger's favorite music plays. It is a moment meant to symbolize the entire memorial. We all hold the strings of our respective balloons, waiting with anticipation in our own thoughts. But the tunes play in absurd fast-forward, no doubt a cassette speed flub, and we all explode into laughter again. It is in every way a Rogerian final act. No amount of slapstick can stop the balloons from being absorbed into autumn azure.

Finally feeling up to talking with Don, I find him leaning back against the wall of the hangar.

'Don, what a great gathering.'

'Yup, I'm sure Roger is happy.'

Don has to fly to the Brooks Range in a few days. I will head to the Kobuk River basin for a caribou shoot. Our respective lives will begin anew.

The fall colors this year are truly splendid. Why is it that even though it is the same season, the hues change subtly each year?

Fall 1993

The Traveling Tree

One day I bump into my friend Lorrie at a woodworking-hardware store in Fairbanks.

'Wow. Has it been two years?' I say. 'What are you doing these days?'

'Working as a carpenter,' she tells me. 'Putting the skills I picked up when I was a kid to good use. Never mind that, though. Do you know how many times I called you in May? I must have rung up everyone in town to ask if they knew where you were! Thought you should know that Bill Pruitt is back in Fairbanks after thirty years. Haven't you been saying for ages that you want to see him?'

Bill Pruitt . . . The name took me way back, to the very first summer after I moved to Alaska. It would have been 1979. I was up on Cape Thompson, a remote headland that juts into the Bering Sea, serving as the lone assistant to ornithologist David G Roseneau for a field survey of seabirds. The bluffs of

Cape Thompson were home to the largest rookery in northern Alaska, including colonies of horned puffins, common murres and black-legged kittiwakes. One stretch of cliff was the nesting ground for golden eagles, and each day I would float with Dave over a swathe of ocean in an inflatable raft to check with binoculars how the chicks were growing. The nearest human habitation was Point Hope, a coastal Inuit village over thirty miles to the north, and we spent our down time tenting in the middle of the great Arctic wilderness.

Accompanying Dave on this expedition yielded many formative experiences. Like my first sighting of a caribou herd, when the two of us dropped onto our bellies in the tundra and intermittently waved handkerchiefs to arouse the animals' curiosity, eventually drawing a few incredibly close. Or the day we were returning from the bluffs at dusk and a grey whale emerged from the sea right beside our boat with a blast of spray. Or the time we found grizzly-bear tracks on the beach but never sighted the grizzly. Spending the first summer of my new life on Cape Thompson was a very gratifying opportunity. It was as though this far-flung realm, cut off from the regular haunts of humankind, were offering me a rite of passage.

Dave had spent his childhood in an Inuit village due to his father's work and, in addition to being well versed in the flora and fauna, he was a spectacular storyteller. When night fell, I would listen to his many tales of the old days in Alaska with the waves of the Arctic Ocean crashing in the background.

I cannot recall how the story of Bill Pruitt came up. Perhaps I had thought it odd that there were rusted old buildings scattered around this small beautiful estuary on an uninhabited headland and decided to ask Dave about it. In any case, Bill and Dave knew each other as fellow biologists. And one night, Dave began to tell me about the role that this estuary played in historic events that once shook Alaska and changed Bill's life forever.

The year was 1960. Led by Edward Teller, the 'father of the hydrogen bomb', the United States Atomic Energy Commission was advancing an experimental plan code-named Project Chariot. The goal was to create an artificial harbor on the northwest coast of Alaska using the explosive power of nuclear bombs. Although no one on the AEC payroll had ever set foot in Alaska, they marked off Cape Thompson on a map; the blighted facilities I was curious about two decades later were the end result.

Bill Pruitt, then a young researcher at the University of Alaska, was among the scientists hired to perform an environmental and safety assessment of the plan. As one of the top field biologists of the day, Bill played a pioneering role in surveys of Alaskan wildlife, inheriting his inexhaustible fascination with the Far North from naturalist Ernest Thompson Seton, who he had read vociferously as a child.

With the backing of unassailable political forces, Project Chariot's approval had been a foregone conclusion from day one. The pressure being exerted on universities was said to have been so great that all researchers tacitly understood that any criticism would cost them their jobs. Nonetheless, Bill stood up against the plan, predicting that it would result in irreversible damage to the natural environment and to nearby Inuit villages. He was eventually dismissed from his academic post, but his actions alerted Inuit peoples to the danger and initiated a massive grassroots protest movement. This was an era of gargantuan national projects all but immune to opposition, and the fight grew protracted. But in the end, in spite of the arguments for its economic benefits, Project Chariot was finally crushed.

Looking back now, this imbroglio was a definitive turning point not only for the state of Alaska in general but for the Inuit of Alaska in particular, as it was the first time in recorded history that their varied communities, dispersed throughout huge tracts of secluded land, had banded together as one people to fight off outside interference.

Bill was forced to leave behind the land that he adored and seek employment at universities in other states, but the AEC ensured that he would never keep his position for long, while the FBI was purportedly tracking his whereabouts. Eventually he abandoned America altogether and immigrated to Canada, where at an advanced age he attained a zoology professorship at the University of Manitoba.

It was a year after I heard Dave's story on Cape Thompson that I realized Bill Pruitt was William Obadiah Pruitt, the author of one of my favorite books, *Animals of the North*. More chronicle of the Alaskan wilderness than standard science textbook, this cult classic of zoology had been out of print once already and I treated my copy with the utmost care.

The first chapter is titled 'The Traveling Tree'. It is the story of a lucky spruce seed knocked to the ground one day in early spring by the careless pecking of a red crossbill that has alighted in its branches. Through a series of chance occurrences, the seed takes root in the woods by a river and grows up to become a great big tree. Over the course of many years, the river erodes its way through the forest until, at last, it is this sizable spruce's turn to stand at the edge of the bank. Then the river overflows in the snowmelt one spring and washes it down the Yukon River to the Bering Sea, where Arctic currents carry it to the shores of the tundra. In this treeless landscape far from the lush region in which it first sprouted, the spruce, now a piece of driftwood, becomes a sort of landmark upon which a fox leaves his territorial scent, but an Inuit hunter stalking the fox soon sets a trap there – and so it continues. The tree's long journey finally concludes inside the woodstove of a cabin in the wilds, only to begin anew as the protagonist is reborn as smoke from the air that the logs consumed.

The evocative redolence of the Far North that permeates every section of this book no doubt contributed to my fascination with the wilderness in these regions. Thirty years later, both its author and the project he was instrumental in stopping have slipped from our collective memory. Until recently when, due to an unexpected development, this all but forgotten history resurfaced.

Just last summer, a librarian at the University of Alaska was examining the Project Chariot records when he came across an old document containing previously undisclosed facts. Despite cancellation of the project, a top-secret experiment had been conducted at Cape Thompson using nuclear waste that had remained buried in the ground ever since. Although the quantity was minuscule, this revelation – the stuff of science fiction – sent the surrounding Inuit communities into a panic and triggered a furor across the state.

This year, yet another piece of news that recalled the controversy reached our ears. The government of Canada had awarded Bill its Northern Science Award Centenary Medal. According to Lorrie, he had been in town this May to visit the University of Alaska for a graduation ceremony, where he had been granted an honorary doctorate. This marked an obvious attempt by the university to apologize some three decades later. But the debt that the wilderness of Alaska and its residents owe him is too great to ever be expressed.

'I filled him in on what you've been up to,' says Lorrie, who was an old friend of Bill's, having grown up in the house next door. 'I told him that some Japanese people love your books.'

Yes, I want to meet Bill if I can. I want to say a word of thanks. Not to the hero that vanquished Project Chariot, but to the naturalist who gave his heart and soul to the North.

When I Was Sixteen

Why did I end up where I am now when I could have made so many other choices? The harder we try to give a simple explanation for our having taken path A over path B, the more the question leaves us stumped. Because the only way to truly answer is to retrace our steps back through all the many crossroads we have confronted over a lifetime.

My first travel experience was a trip to the USA when I was sixteen years old. Unlike today when going abroad is commonplace, America back then seemed like a remote and alien country all the way beyond the incalculably broad waters of the Pacific Ocean. But ever since I was in middle school, I had nursed a secret desire to cross that ocean by boat and hitchhike across the country like a nomad. Often during class, I would feel my blood warm as I gazed out the window envisioning this journey. What adventure surely awaited me in America.

I wanted to break out of the coddled everyday and touch that thing they call the world.

I had already decided which friend I would take with me. One day as our graduation ceremony approached, I called him over to a corner of the school grounds and told him about my plan. I had been working it all out in my head for a long time and this moment was meant to be one for the history books. But things didn't go quite as I had expected. When my friend was supposed to say, 'Sounds great, let's do it!' he just gaped at me as if paralyzed. In retrospect, it was only natural that he would react that way. At the time, I was crestfallen. It was as though the strength were draining from my whole body. I can still remember that feeling clearly, twenty-five years later.

From then on, all I could think about was going alone. So after I started high school, I found a part-time job and began to save up money. I followed up on leads from acquaintances and made preparations, visiting the Port of Yokohama to consult with the crews of international freighters. I was hoping they might have a dishwashing job for me.

When I mentioned my plan to my parents and others around me, they didn't take me seriously. In those days, the very idea that a sixteen-year-old upstart like me might travel by his or herself around America was too outrageous to even oppose. But as childish as I may have been, I wasn't playing around about this. In the end, there was just one person who was willing to finally hear me out: my father. He told me that if I really wanted to go, he would put up the cash. For a salaryman like him, it was no small sum. And he was placing a bet that would no doubt undermine his parenting credentials in the eyes of many. After all, what if I didn't make it back in one piece? That is just how superlatively far any country outside Japan seemed back then.

In the summer of 1968, I boarded the *Argentina Maru*, a liner bound for Brazil that had for many years carried migrants, and embarked from the Port of Yokohama. Having a cross-ocean voyage as my first trip ever gave me a visceral sense of the scale of our planet. The vast blue of the Pacific overawed me. Every night I would go above deck to listen to the rolling waves and gaze at stars that seemed to rain upon me. Spending day after day with nothing in sight but the sea, I was seized with the impression that the land upon which I had lived was an unstable and fleeting refuge while these fathomless waters were the genuine reality of the Earth. The ocean was gently teaching me the boundlessness of imagination and the brevity of a human life.

Two weeks later, the city of Los Angeles – our port of arrival in America – appeared on the horizon. My only possession was the large American army-surplus backpack slung on my shoulders. It was stuffed full of such essentials as a tent, sleeping bag, portable gas stove and map of the USA.

The dreary outlying port was largely deserted and dusk was falling. I knew no one, had nowhere to sleep that night and had made no plans. All there was for me to do was roll the dice and head north or south. Without curfew or anyone who knew where I was, it was the most refreshing experience a budding soul like mine could have hoped for. Untroubled by even the slightest unease, my chest filled with a kind of tenderness at the freedom that made me want to scream and holler.

There was nowhere to pitch tent in LA, so I spent the night at a cheap guesthouse on the edge of town. It doubled as an apartment inhabited by all manner of strange folk, and my first night in America was a raucous one, punctuated by unidentified shouts and shrieks.

I know now that this was a tumultuous decade for America, disturbed as it was by ghetto riots, the Vietnam War and the assassinations of both Martin Luther King and President John F Kennedy. But ignorant of such social problems and lacking any fear of crime, I began my rove through that nation in simple euphoria.

On one day, I arrived just before sundown at the Grand Canyon, its enormity overturning my former sense of nature's magnitude. This first night tenting in a truly expansive landscape planted a seed in my mind – a seed that seems to have sprouted and grown slowly, transforming into a yearning for Alaska.

I decided that when I arrived in New York I would go hear Peter, Paul and Mary – or PPM as the American folk group was known in Japan, where they were then quite popular. I even had the fanciful notion that I might go meet them and have a chat if the opportunity presented itself. I now recall with wistful embarrassment hauling out to Greenwich Village to inquire at their office.

The southern cities I visited by Greyhound – Atlanta, Nashville, New Orleans – were intense. I would step off the bus and find myself immersed in the societies of black people. The multifarious aroma of the bus stations, combining such scents as toilet, shoe polish, hot dog and hamburger, even now evokes for me the America of long ago. Then there were the sunsets and sunrises I watched from the bus while it drove across the plains.

I exchanged words and then parted with all sorts of people each and every day. Somehow what should have been obvious – the fact that there are countless people out there in the world – struck me as something mysterious.

Along the way, I made a major course change and dipped down to Mexico, touring the ruins of ancient civilizations on an excursion to the tip of the Yucatan Peninsula. One night I lost my way in the small town of Mérida and could not escape from a maze of sketchy alleyways however long I walked, only making it back to my lodging after a passing cop car picked me up. Even in my youthful naivety, I was not immune to the stress of danger.

Later a family gave me a ride while I was hitchhiking in Canada. I traveled with them for ten days and they remain like a second family to me even twenty-five years later. I paid a visit last year for the first time in ages to the mother and father, who live in the city of Edmonton, and we reminisced about that trip. The daughter Belinda, then seven, had become a Canadian actor with her own distinctive style, while the son Donald, then twelve, was a documentary-film cameraman.

'That day, when we passed Michio by while he was hitchhiking on the highway,' the aging mother recalled, 'Belinda kept insisting, "Go back again and pick him up."'

Encountering and receiving the helping hands of many people, I safely completed my two-month trip. The day I arrived in San Francisco, my final destination, I toasted myself with a Coca-Cola and a super-sized hamburger. If the mind had such a thing as muscles, I would have felt them working inside me like never before.

Looking back, I think sixteen was a touch too young. Pushing all five senses to the limit and putting everything I had into just surviving day to day, I didn't have the space to properly observe and take in the many things I perceived. Still, those days remain the most exhilarating of my life. Being alone ensured that I would never run out of new people to meet and that the thrill of danger was never far away. The most curious aspect of it all, though, was how the decisions I made each day unlocked new events. It was as though I were living a story with no script. Missing a single bus meant that an entirely different set of experiences awaited. If you get right down to it, this is the very essence of life and of human encounters – a truth I understood vividly thanks to that trip.

In some sense, I had taken a vacation from reality. Back home after it was all over, my routine as a Japanese high-school student was there waiting for me unchanged. But I returned to it with a sense of emancipation and relief, having grasped the enormity of the world. There was so much more out there than just the place I lived. A multitude of people in distant foreign lands with a multitude of values and beliefs were living out their lives just as I was. That is, the journey had given me for the first time a relativizing perspective on the society in which I had been raised and now had to make my way. This was a major evolution within me. For in my fascination with scenes of Alaska's diverse peoples, I seem to be recapitulating the same process of seeing anew.

Life in Alaska

A new day in early spring, a Sunday no less, begins with the two of us rushing about the house. Never have we sent out invitations for an 'official' party at our home before.

Not that we're expecting it be a suit and tie affair. This is Alaska after all. You can turn up just about anywhere in jeans or rain boots and no one will bat an eye. People here have little interest in such things as appearances or titles. Their childlike curiosity is more likely to be piqued by someone who has cast off these pretensions. Presumably this will all be true of the reception we are holding today for my friends in Fairbanks who missed our wedding in Japan last month.

Naoko and I string balloons on the silver birches in the entrance, ready the bonfire for the salmon roast and finish setting the tables both inside and out. I wonder how much we have left to do. Probably a lot – because if you include the children, we'll be hosting close to a hundred guests today.

One of my main intentions in holding the reception is to introduce Naoko as quickly as possible to as many of my Alaska friends as I can. I figure that if she's going to adjust and learn to love the land, she'll need to become acquainted with the people. But as a newcomer, she still struggles to speak English and has built up the event into an object of significant anxiety.

'Don't worry about it; no one is expecting you to be fluent right away,' I say, giving her an emergency pep talk. 'But they will be looking for signs of whether you're really making an effort to become a part of Alaska. Even if you don't understand what they're saying, might be important to smile, okay?'

I have a more personal reason for holding this reception as well, something I want to settle concerning my relationship with the people here. It's surely thanks to their assistance that I've come this far. Over the fifteen years since I moved here from Japan, I have encountered so many new faces; and somewhere along the way, I began to ask myself where I truly wanted to be. My eventual decision to settle in Alaska resulted in several momentous changes for me. One was buying land and building a house a few years ago – thereby putting an end to my days in a cabin with no running water or toilet, if not to my wandering ways. Another was marrying my wife. I suppose these were my ways of shouting out, 'Okay, I'm really going to start living here, you hear me, Alaska!'

This transition to settling here for good also brought about a gradual shift in my perspective on the natural world that encompasses me. The wilderness had heretofore felt removed, like some spectacular movie for which I had purchased tickets.

Now my connection to it has been subtly redefined. My own brief life and the brief lives of the wolves I cross paths with in the wilds have become somehow intertwined. So too other wildlife. So too other people. Now I want to cherish what this new outlook has allowed me to perceive.

With the arrival of evening (if you can call it that during the season of polar nights, with the sun as high as in daytime), our guests stream in. It is delightful and amusing to see that everyone – out of step with local custom – is dressed up. We have set up the reception as a potluck, with everyone bringing one dish to share.

Fred Dean, a professor from when I studied at the University of Alaska's Department of Biology and Wildlife, arrives with his wife Susan. Fred is a specialist in bears, and I used to accompany him annually to observe grizzlies at Denali National Park. Then five years ago, Susan had surgery for cancer and Fred moved out of fieldwork, no doubt overcome with worry. But this spring, I caught sight of him in the mountains around Denali, scouting for bears with binoculars as in days past. I'm relieved to find Susan looking well today too.

My indigenous friend Al climbs the street with his wife Gay and their kids in tow. I can't remember the last time I saw him. The two of us have been friends since our commencement ceremony. The sight of him lining up that day at the office for the Department of Biology and Wildlife is still etched in my memory. Going on forty, and with shoulder-length hair and moose-hide clothes, Al openly telegraphed that he was indigenous. Sensing our affinity, we became instant friends.

During my journeys through Alaska from then on, Al always stood at the entrance to unknown worlds and opened the door if I wanted to peek inside. Then there was his wedding in his village along the Yukon River on that glorious autumn day. I had my concerns about whether things would work out between him, an indigenous man raised in the Alaskan wilds, and Gay, a white woman raised in New York. But a new life bearing two cultures had already taken hold inside her; and look how big he is now.

I have always loved Al's gentle gaze, steadily witnessing the movement of all phenomena. While we are excitedly catching up, I glance skyward to find clouds that look ready to burst.

'It would really suck if it rained today,' I mutter.

'Not to worry, Michio,' he tells me. 'Rain falls when it falls and stops when it stops.'

His words tenderly conjure our past together. How often has he helped me to stop fretting the small stuff?

Alfred, not to be confused with Al, has come all the way from the city of Delta Junction. We met when my engine stalled out on the Alaska Highway, leaving me stranded in the hinterlands on a terrifyingly cold winter day, with temperatures dropping to nearly minus forty. Alfred happened to be passing along the road and took the rest of the day off work to help me, a complete stranger, towing my car to the nearest town some hundred and twenty-five miles away. He even let me stay in his house for three days until the repairs were complete. We've been like family ever since.

Don Ross arrives. Then an Inuit named Mabel, who I go blueberry-picking with in fall, and her (I'd guess) eighty-year-old mother Suzy. The grave of Suzy's deceased husband Simon Paneak, a conduit of oral stories from times past, has been laid out together with that of ethnologist Masao Oka in the wilds of Anaktuvuk Pass as per the wills of the two men. The story of their friendship is quite beautiful.

Watching the spectacle of numerous people arriving in succession sends me into a strange revery. It's like a flashback in fast-forward of my fifteen-year journey through Alaska.

Just as I feared, rain begins to fall. The hundred-odd guests cram into our small house, transforming the reception into a freewheeling Alaska-style shindig. They sit chatting on our stairs and throng the entrance and kitchen and around the woodburning stove. It's my first house party and I'm not at all used to this. But I'm happy.

Everyone has words of encouragement for Naoko on her fresh arrival from Japan. I expect that they're a little concerned about the complete one-eighty she is doing with her life, leaving behind the flash and sparkle of the big city for this most harsh of winters. So many things that we hardened Alaskans take as a matter of course will be startlingly new for her. At this moment, she is trying her best to understand a carefully enunciated lecture from my cameraman friend Kim.

'Listen to me, Naoko, here's a piece of advice,' Kim says, speaking at a geologically slow pace and repeating everything twice. 'Being cold warms people's hearts. Being apart draws people together.'

Listening intently, my wife brightens into a smile. Something tells me she'll do just fine here.

Inborn River

Scenes of human life are intriguing by virtue of a commonality that puts everyone on the same playing field. The commonality I refer to is the wish shared by all alike for their one and only life to be the best it can be. What makes this intriguing is how the infinitely diverse ways to live ramify from each of those many wishes.

One early-spring day, I head off to visit my old friend Bill Fuller at his home in Fairbanks. There's never anything I *have* to discuss with Bill, who turns seventy-five this year, but I nevertheless find myself wanting to meet him now and again. If a human being is the sort of organism that needs occasional encouragement as a matter of survival, then Bill is most certainly the person who gives that to me. Whenever I stumble, all I have to do is look at Bill's face and I know exactly how to pick myself back up again.

It's not as if our hero Bill Fuller has some great accomplishment to his name. He possesses no titles to speak of. But Bill is the real deal. Which may be precisely what makes Bill a true hero – a hero exclusively for those who know him.

On a winter day in Fairbanks, you can crank the heat in your car to the max and still be cold. Even so, you will see an old man pedaling your way on his bicycle, just sailing along through minus-forty-degree air.

'When it drops to minus thirty,' Bill once told me, 'bicycle tires have fantastic traction on snow.'

In the vicinity of twenty below zero, Bill wears flip-flops on bare feet even outside. This is not some show of endurance, nor does he practice cold-resistance training.

'You're really not cold?' I once asked, utterly appalled.

'I've been like this ever since I was a kid,' he explained. 'You might say my circulation is good, or at least my extremities are hotter than most folks.'

In his late sixties, Bill took up Japanese, memorizing over six hundred kanji. Then he went on a trip suited for a student in their twenties, cycling from Hokkaido to Kyushu before returning home. The Japanese people he met en route must have been in awe of the old man with a spirit as free as the wind. I know firsthand just how uplifting time spent with Bill is for those fortunate enough to have made his acquaintance.

I've never come across an elderly couple who live as simply as Bill and his wife Nancy. Even in this city, where you will still frequently hear people say they want running water when they get married, Bill and Nancy are about the only over-seventies who do without it. Furnishing their kitchen is a small water tank, filled up from what source I do not know. Survey the interior of their house – a mere two hundred and seventy square feet – and Bill's lifestyle bespeaks the scant belongings a human being truly needs. In other words, Bill is a paragon of living light. Which reminds me of a phrase I once heard: 'personal definition of success'. Bill demonstrates that there are extremely individualistic notions of success and failure in life at the utmost distance from society's yardstick.

Born in Massachusetts in 1919, Bill walked many different paths before finding his way to Alaska. Taking an interest in celestial navigation at a young age, he embarked on an ocean-going merchant vessel and later served as a navigator for Pan American Airways in the early days when they had just begun to fly by the stars. After World War II, he worked alongside Mexican farmhands on sugarcane plantations in the South and put the nimbleness of his hands to use as a sailmaker in California. Then there is the story of when his talent for dance was recognized after many years of lessons, and he was given a chance to appear on stage in New York only to forfeit it after he broke a bone while skiing. Bill is also drawn to academic study and has a master's degree in plant pathology from the University of California.

A truly multifaceted career. While everyone else strives to accomplish something, Bill has always led his life just as it is. Perhaps this is to make your way within the current of your inborn river. Bill certainly seems to think so.

'I think everyone gets along like that in the beginning,' he said. 'But at a startlingly young age they abandon that current and try to reach the shore.'

After his first visit to Alaska in 1970, Bill was thoroughly enchanted and decided to settle here. Together with Nancy, who had been a social worker, he found various employments in a far-flung town out in the wilds. I met Bill after he and Nancy were emancipated from these manifold labors and had retired to Fairbanks.

Even now, he volunteers as a teacher of music for kindergarteners and of ESL for University of Alaska international students, is a fixture at the social dance gatherings in town, and continues to practice Spanish and Japanese on his own with great gusto. While aging tends to make us more conservative in a material and monetary sense, Bill takes the opposite approach with his energy and invests it all in the present.

What endears Bill to me is the severity and sadness concealed deep within his gentle but animated eyes. His has certainly not been an uneventful life of fun and games. There were the deaths of a child he will never speak of and of his beloved younger brother, left in a wheelchair after a tragic accident. Looking at Bill makes me think that the depth of our aging depends upon how many crossroads we have stood at in life and how dearly we have held our many sorrows.

When I turn onto Cloudberry Lane and enter the black spruce forest in which Bill's house is found, the path becomes bumpy. Fresh green is almost here. I spot Nancy walking with plates in her arms, apparently returning from the house of a neighbor.

'Is Bill around?' I ask.

'Oh, long time no see,' says Nancy. 'Bill is in his room studying Spanish. I'm sure he'll be happy to see you!'

The road narrows further, and several log cabins reminiscent of the pioneer era can be seen inside the forest. The area is full of young people living in true Alaska style. Judging by the way they interact with Bill, I can't think of any old person better at slipping through generational divides. In the forest is a communal volleyball net. During the season of the midnight sun, local residents play here until around 1am every Wednesday. I've been invited to join several times. Bill is of course a key regular.

Bill and Nancy's small house is located at the dead end deep in the forest. Nancy's modest vegetable garden. The simple shower of sun-heated rainwater. The hand-me-down bicycle that has been Bill's sole mode of transportation for the past half a dozen years . . . Bill's study is on the second floor of their newly built storage shed. Surrounded by spruce and entered from the outside by ladder-like stairs, it has the feel of a treehouse.

'Hey, Bill, it sure has been a while!'

'Hi there, Michio. Nice of you to stop by.'

'I hear you're working on your Spanish.'

That sadness-tinged smile of his always puts me at ease. The May breeze blowing in through the window flips the pages of the dictionary and textbook on Bill's desk. Around the feeders hung from spruce branches, boreal chickadees and redpolls flit about, twittering songs of early spring. The season has turned again.

Although Bill has slowed down on his Japanese study now, he was obsessed until recently. I can't help wondering what on earth he will get out of it given how much time remains to him.

'*Haru ga kimashita*,' Bill says in halting Japanese – 'spring has come' – and begins to write the characters down as if to confirm something.

'Michio, what is the kanji for *haru* again?'

Even if I knew that tomorrow the world would go to pieces, I would still plant my apple tree today. Bill's existence always poses the question to me of why we should try to affirm life.

Caribou Soup

Inside the cabin of a Cessna, I sit balancing a container of caribou soup carefully in both hands. Occasional patches of turbulence shake the small plane, and I adjust my parcel as best I can so as not to spill. But judging from the faint scent that wafts through the confined space, a small amount has already escaped from the lid.

I'm on my way back to Fairbanks from the Arctic village of Ambler, where I have been staying with an Inuit friend and his family. Just before takeoff, he asked me to bring the soup to his daughter, who is studying in the city at my old alma mater, the University of Alaska. It is still warm to the touch.

I press my face up to the glass of the window and gaze down on the wilds spread out below, recalling something that happened in days gone by. This must have been fifteen years ago, when I was still in college.

The superintendent of the dorm I lived in contacted me one day to ask if an Inuit student could move in with me. Apparently he never got along well with his previous roommate, who was white, and had now finally stormed out. Inuit and other indigenous people made up twenty percent of the student body at the University of Alaska, and since room allocations were decided randomly, they frequently ended up living with white students. Unfortunately, the cramped rooms of the dorm did not appear suited to the cohabitation of strangers raised in such radically different ways, as this arrangement often led to conflict.

The Inuit boy who walked bashfully through the door of my room one day with a Boston bag slung over his shoulder was called Willard. The moment he saw me, something in him seemed to relax. Our backgrounds were admittedly different – I was from a suburb of Tokyo while he was from an inland Inuit village in the Alaskan wilderness – but my face, which might be mistaken for North American indigenous due to the ancient east Asian ancestry we share, appeared to put him at ease.

Once Willard and I began rooming together, we found ourselves gradually becoming friends. Whenever he received one the packages of food his parents occasionally sent, he always made sure to divvy out a portion for me. Sometimes it would be smoked salmon, cranberries or the dried meat of moose and caribou – the white substance crammed in a bottle was lard made from bears. This he would scoop up with his fingers and eat like it was some delectable treat. Every time his supplies arrived, I could almost feel the wind of the seasons blowing through his village.

After some time had passed, Willard told me that he wanted to drop out of school and return home. Stopping short of graduation in this way is common for indigenous students; often they have trouble adjusting to the new environment or are unable to keep up with their classes.

'You've come this far,' I said. 'Why not stick it out a bit longer?'

But despite my efforts to encourage him, Willard packed up suddenly one day and left for his village. I heard nothing from him until a week later when I received a call at the dorm.

'I just got back from the hunt,' he said. 'I caught a bear . . .'

Willard had never been much of a talker, but he had gone to the trouble of ringing me up just to tell me that. The sound of his voice called to mind a bird released from its cage, and I began to think that maybe leaving had been the right choice for him after all.

'I'm definitely going to visit you someday,' I said.

'Sure. We'll be happy to have you any time.'

Standing in the silent hallway of the dorm, I could sense the vastness of the wilderness on the other end of the receiver.

Not long after, I began to travel through Alaska and visit many communities, where I learned about the cultures of hunting peoples that were until then unknown to me. I remember one occasion when I was standing with a group of Inuit on an ice floe in the Bering Sea, watching a massive flock of king eiders migrating from the south. While I was enthralled by the beautiful formation in which these sea ducks flew, signaling the arrival of spring, my companions were licking their lips, guns at the ready, their heads filled with the long-awaited taste of duck soup. This gap in our perceptions of nature seemed curious to me, and I found myself growing ever more fascinated by their perspective.

One event that left a deep impression on me was the whale hunt that I witnessed in Point Hope. Through patches of freezing seawater that filled great cracks in ice sheets, the villagers paddled seal-skinned *umiaks* in pursuit of their leviathan quarry. It was an unforgettable experience that I cannot fully capture in words. What struck me most of all was the sacredness with which they imbued the whales they killed, giving a prayer before butchering the body and then performing the ritual of returning the leftover skull to the sea. Other cultural practices I observed, including the caribou and moose hunt, offered similar glimpses of the way in which they interacted with nature.

Although phrases like 'wildlife conservation' and 'animal welfare' have never had any pull for me, I have reflected for many years on the paradigm of hunting peoples and believe that their mode of interaction with nature holds a crucial lesson. The point I wish to explore concerns the contingency that all hunting peoples have no choice but to embrace. One example is the ice-sheet cracks just mentioned, which are known as 'leads' and which are all-important for the Inuit whale hunt. Leads form in the spring when the frozen surface of the Bering Sea gradually begins to fracture due to the force of currents and wind. For the hunt to occur, the leads cannot be either too big or too small, and yet the ice shifts constantly, often closing them up before your eyes. In other words, only when a particular constellation of natural conditions comes together in just the right way does the whale hunt first become possible, and this fundamental predicament is presumably common to all hunting peoples. Moreover, the contingency intrinsic to the hunting way of life inculcates hunting peoples with a certain kind of spiritual reality, expressed in the belief that human existence is in some sense sustained by that which lies outside us. Is this not the unconscious frame of mind that comes into play in such primal interactions as the encounter with a moose in a forest or the launching of a harpoon at a whale?

To remain in existence is to make the unending daily choice of who to sacrifice in order that you may survive, as the essence of all sentient beings is the killing and eating of the other. While this covenant is obscured within modern life, hunting peoples must confront it head-on without flinching. 'Covenant' refers to 'the scent of blood' and is synonymous with 'sorrow' – the same sorrow from which the myths of ancient times must surely have arisen.

Through ceremonies and gifts for the animals they slay, hunters propitiate their spirits and pray that they will return to become the sacrificed once more. In this way they pay heed to the unspoken sadness that is a law of our world. Unless and until we can do the same, no amount of trekking through mountains and fields or pondering in our armchairs will ever yield true understanding of the relationship between humanity and nature. By taking the life of the other who inhabits our land and filling ourselves with its blood, human beings form a deeper connection to the Earth. And perhaps our mental separation from nature can be traced to the moment we ceased to engage in such acts.

My reminiscing is cut short when the Cessna touches down in Fairbanks. This caribou-soup delivery service has crossed over three hundred miles of wilderness. I immediately call my friend's daughter.

'Jennifer, I've just come back from Ambler with something your father asked me to bring you. Can you guess what it is?'

On the other end of the line, Jennifer thinks it over for a while. The meat in the soup is from a caribou caught by her brother Alvin. By now it has gone completely cold, but I am certain it will still replenish Jennifer's body with the blood of the wilds she longs for.

People of the Beaver

I feel the sun's warmth on my forehead as I lean it against the glass of the Cessna's window. The newly thawed Yukon River snakes and sparkles across the land. I doubt anyone has ever stood beside the countless lakes and marshes scattered below me; they don't even have names. Nature existing for its own sake, unconnected to the reality of humankind. I have long been fascinated by the meaningless expanse that Alaska contains.

A perennial speculation occupies me. What if Anglo-Saxons had never come to North America? What if the continent had been set apart for the Inuit and other indigenous peoples, isolated from the rest of the world? Would they have one day constructed modernity like ours? Are human ways of life destined to proceed along the same course, albeit at different speeds? There is little point in contemplating such alternatives, as history is a process that unfolds only once – we cannot pick and choose it retroactively. And yet I am seized by these imaginings whenever my thoughts turn to the cultures of those who lived in harmony with nature, prior to contact with the modern world, just one or two generations ago.

The Cessna crosses the Yukon. We are headed to Chalkyitsik, where I'm scheduled to meet with an eighty-two-year-old man named David Salmon. It is the first Athabascan village I will visit as part of a plan with my friend Walter Newman to speak with various elders over the next two years. We feel it our duty to listen to the stories of the people before they fade away.

With a population of some one hundred residents, Chalkyitsik is located on the bank of Black River, which flows from the Brooks Range. The name means 'fishhook' in the local language, suggesting longstanding abundance of freshwater catch. In contrast to the modern-style houses that have unfortunately been adopted by Inuit communities, the village follows many inland indigenous settlements in consisting mostly of small log cabins, offering visitors a beautiful scene.

David Salmon is a chief and a spiritual leader of the people, occupying the second most important rank among Alaskan Athabascans. I like this elder as soon as I lay eyes on him. He has warm eyes that remain fixed on whomever he is speaking with and a face that projects the dignity of his character. It is also the face of someone who has survived an era. We will be staying with David in his cabin, where he has lived alone since his wife's passing.

The distribution of Alaska Natives can be divided roughly into Athabascans, who inhabit the interior, and Inuit, who inhabit the coasts. Walter is of Inuit blood though raised in the Athabascan village of Beaver. I learned this when he told me of Frank Yasuda, a Japanese man who in 1907 led an Inuit village stricken by famine on a two-year-long journey across the Arctic barrens to the location inside Athabascan lands of present-day Beaver. Walter has committed the epic tale to memory like a true storyteller, having heard it from his aging father, who partook in the exodus when he was a child. Yasuda was still in Beaver as an old man during Walter's childhood there, and I expect that my friend's knowledge about and interest in the history of his people comes from his experience knowing the man.

'David, speak with me,' Walter says. It is a phrase he uses as a sort of greeting with old people. I always find it kind of strange, though it must have been a crucial feature of life long ago.

In this season when the sun does not set, we listen closely to David. It is one of those summer nights of the Far North in which the flow of time seems to stop. Even past midnight, we hear the voices of the children and other villagers.

'. . . Since the distant past, we Indians have only thought about three things: Earth, animals and people. For the purpose of survival, you see. Wealth – no one paid any mind to such a thing. And we were split into three tribes. The Best Indians, the Medium Indians and the Slave Indians. I have Slave Indian blood. The Best Indians are the ones who originally came to this land long long ago, and the color of their skin was always dark. They gave all orders that mattered to survival and people obeyed.'

'How long is long long ago? Where did they come from?'

'Thousands and thousands of years. They came from Siberia.'

David is the first person I have met who knows the prehistoric plains of Beringia now sunken beneath the sea not as some dry fact but within his body.

'Were the Best Indians the richest? I mean, was there such a thing as class?'

'No. Wealth has nothing to do with it. When people were at a crossroads and didn't know what to do to survive, they were the ones who decided which direction to take.'

I lose count of how many times I hear the word 'survive' in David's stories.

'In order to survive, people lived with their eyes always on animals, and they changed depending on the animal they caught and lived off. The movement of the Indians of Old Crow is like the caribou. You can see it right away when they dance. The Indians of the Yukon River are the strongest. This is because they have eaten the king salmon who swims against the rapids. I am one of the people of the beaver. Haven't you noticed that the villagers of Chalkyitsik speak softly? This is because we have eaten and lived like the beaver.'

I recall the beaver carcass inside the storeroom by the entrance to his cabin.

'In olden times people wandered in search of animals. On cold winter journeys, it was fast runners who would carry the fire. When we were going to change our campsite, one of us would go on ahead, making preparations for many fires along the way. And when everyone set off, the fast ones would retrieve a torch from the embers and run with it to the site of the next fire. In this way, we traveled to the next campsite carrying the fire along little by little. You can start fire with a rock rubbed against the powder taken from stems of cottonwood, but it's hard work in minus-fifty-degree cold. That is why we carried fire with great care once we had it.'

One afternoon, David's seven-year-old granddaughter Cheri comes to play. David tells her old stories while seated in his chair.

'In the distant past, there was a girl who survived a war between tribes. You know the valley called Igloo Creek on the other side of the mountains, don't you? That girl began to live there catching fish all by herself.'

Cheri is a child of the modern world but still she listens intently. I am riveted by the scene. Will Cheri pass on the tale she hears today to her own children when she becomes a mother?

'I'll come again, Grandpa!' she says excitedly. From the way she runs out of the cabin, I can sense how she reveres this elder in her own childlike way. So concludes a mysterious moment in which one who will depart and one who will strive to live on have crossed paths.

Atop the hill at the edge of the village, I see across the unending wilds of early spring all the way to the horizon. Vast untouched nature . . . The pristine expanses of this land that enchanted me now appear different. All I have done is meet a single Athabascan elder and already the landscape

is beginning to tell me something. The northlands I felt to be
pure of human visitation had in truth been crisscrossed by
myriad peoples. With the pleasant wind of the Far North on
my skin, I recall a passage from a book I once read:

> All matter is fossil, and it is not ancient only once . . .
> When a breeze envelopes your body, think of it as an
> old story blowing on you. For the wind is a true fossil of
> unbelievable softness.

One Family's Journey

I receive a letter from Pat McCormick for the first time in ages.

> Hi Michio, how are you doing? I'm currently on a road
> trip around the USA. I'm still unsure where I'll end up
> living, but I hope to decide by fall. Kevin was very happy
> to meet you at your photo exhibition in Pittsburgh.

Already a year has gone by since Pat left Alaska. Aside from
her daughter Karen, who works in-state as a veterinarian,
all of her kids have moved to mainland America. Her second
son Kevin has completed his PhD at Cornell University and
become a brilliant young chemist.

I met the McCormicks fifteen years ago. I remember
because I had just moved to Alaska that year.

It was the time of year when the fall colors are so vivid
they practically sting your eyes. I was in the mountains of

Denali National Park when I came across a wolf, my first-ever sighting. The animal quickly disappeared into a valley, and while I was following after it, lugging my heavy backpack, I ran into two young men.

'I just saw a wolf around here,' I said.

'Yeah, so did we,' one of them replied. 'I guess we were following the same wolf.'

We then sheepishly introduced ourselves. They were brothers, Paul and Kevin, who had very recently moved to Alaska with their family from the state of Massachusetts. The one who had spoken was the elder brother Kevin. He would be returning to Fairbanks that day for the University of Alaska's fall term. I had also just started at the school.

'What program are you in?' I asked.

'The Department of Biology and Wildlife,' he said.

'What? Me too!'

And so it was that I connected with the McCormicks. Kevin and I ended up taking the same class and gradually became friends. Unlike the other students, who could be rough around the edges, Kevin was somewhat shy, exuding a refined and laid-back air. I took it for the temperament of an eastern US conservative. Only later would I learn what extraordinary aptitude the McCormicks possessed. In addition to biology and wildlife, Kevin would also major in chemistry and graduate at the top of his class in both programs. Strangely enough, however, Kevin showed no signs that he cared in the slightest about grades. Whenever he and Paul had free time, they would put on their backpacks and head out into nature.

I believe that the whole family, Kevin included, came to Alaska searching for something.

The impression of hardheadedness I got from the mother Pat troubled me in the beginning, but we eventually became close friends. When I came back from long photo shoots, I would often go to the McCormick house for dinner and regale them with my travels. Pat would always listen with a sparkle in her eye. Meanwhile, she had started to dip her toes in the Alaskan wilderness herself. Kevin and Paul assisted her in this process of discovery, taking her camping in the Arctic tundra to see the caribou migration. For a woman who was supposed to spend her life as a mother in an eastern American conservative home, I'm certain this was a grand adventure.

Last winter, I held an exhibition of my photos in the eastern city of Pittsburgh for the first time and saw a familiar face at the opening party. Kevin had hurried over all the way from New York with his wife. Newly married, they looked happy. He had taken after his father and begun a career as a chemist. He was as shy as ever.

The two of us reminisced about old times, recalling that autumn day when we had met while chasing a wolf. Seven years had passed since Kevin moved to New York, and Alaska had already become for him somewhere separate and faraway. But I suspect that the natural world had endowed each of the McCormicks, Kevin no less than Pat, with their own respective kind of strength. He told me that Pat was currently traveling, looking for a new place to settle down. It seemed like the beginning of a new era in the family saga.

I'm very sad that I couldn't make it to your photo exhibition, but Kevin told me all about it by letter. All my kids have begun to walk their own paths in life, which reminds me. I visited Africa for the first time this spring, though on a tour. The natural world there is different than in Alaska. Still, I saw plenty of wildlife . . . I imagine you're busy with your photography work as always, but please take care. Once I decide on the place I'll be living, I'll let you know. Yours

The Eskimo Olympics

Every July in downtown Fairbanks, the World Eskimo-Indian Olympics* are held. Crowds gather from villages across Alaska to compete at a variety of traditional sports and games. It is a very silly kind of Olympics, including such events as a tug-of-war with a thread tied to the ears and a high kick to send a ball the highest. But the traditional Inuit dances performed by each village are what serve as the main attraction. At night, thousands throng the enormous indoor venue. In addition to Inuit, the crowd is made up of many Fairbanksers, residents of elsewhere in the state and tourists from mainland America. This four-day annual gathering is a chance for Alaska Natives to both affirm and promote their cultural identities.

---

* Established in 1961, the W EIO remains an annual multi-sport event competed in by indigenous peoples.

On the morning of the first day one year, I receive a phone call from an old friend.

'That Milligrock? Yup. It's me, Earl! Earl Kingik!'

Earl is a man I once accompanied whale hunting. He's currently visiting Fairbanks with a group from Point Hope, the village where I was given the Inuit name Milligrock many moons ago.

'I've been looking you up in the phonebook all morning. It was a tough search. I couldn't remember your last name!'

I burst out laughing into the receiver. Finding my number must have taken ages.

'Point Hope is dancing tonight. Come watch us rehearse this afternoon at the University of Alaska. John and Molly really want to see you too. Wow, Milligrock! See you then.'

This is where in English we would say 'it made my day'. The human heart can be so easily fulfilled by the smallest things. Someone you met long ago misses you. What could make anyone happier than that?

It's been thirteen years now since I joined in the Inuit whale hunt at Point Hope. I've done plenty of traveling in my life, but that was the most intense experience I have ever had. Various scenes from that month have sedimented firmly in my recollection, but one night in particular remains especially vivid.

From the distance of the Arctic Ocean waters that fill a huge fracture in the sea ice, a lone bowhead whale came slowly in our direction , blowing its spout into the air as it went. All of us in the camp held our breath atop the ice and stared at that single approaching point. The uncanny hues of the midnight sun tinged the universe of ice that encompassed us, a full moon hanging in the firmament above. Lined up along the edge of the lead every hundred yards were *umiaks*. Men hid alongside the gunwales of these sealskin boats, still, as though they too were frozen. Time stopped; all that moved in our world was the obliviously approaching whale. What I will never forget is the silence, a deep silence in which you could almost hear the leviathan's breathing. As though choreographed in advance, several dozen *umiaks* slid into the water in unison. These many shadows converged soundlessly through the luminous sea. It was beautiful, unbearably beautiful, the endeavors of those tiny people moving within the giant receptacle of nature.

Earl was the one who gave me the opportunity to join the whale hunt. Outsiders were not usually allowed but he negotiated with the village elders to let him take me. Earl is an idiosyncratic and fiercely individual man. Still, I sense in his expression, gaze and mannerisms the blood of the Inuit flowing generation to generation from the distant past.

That afternoon, Naoko and I go out to the rehearsal space at the University of Alaska. Earl only just learned on the phone that we were married last year and that I would soon be a father. Even before we open the door, I hear a fierce drumbeat. Some two dozen of the villagers are singing, dancing and beating on traditional drums. Once we have stepped among the spectators, I survey the performers from a short distance away and spot Earl waving.

Naoko and I slip quietly into our seats so as not to interfere with the rehearsal. John Oktollik and his beloved wife

Molly are here. John, a village elder who was captain of the whale hunt, notices me right away and begins whispering something to Molly. I spot two young representatives of the next generation, Ernest and Peter. It's so great to see them after all these years.

The Inuit dance rehearsal is conducted with strictness even amid laughter, elders relentlessly calling out advice to the children. Point Hope is known for having the most powerful dancers of any village in Alaska.

Earl stands up abruptly. He looks as if he's about to dance solo. I never knew him to be the dancing type. Pivoting around to face us, he raises his hands high into the air and yells, 'Michio, this dance is for you!'

With everyone's eyes on me suddenly, I squirm in my seat. As Earl's vigorous movements and the beat played on sealskin come into concord, and he begins to caper around the spacious floor, it is as if my friend has transformed into an animal amid the singing of the villagers. The energy surging from his body, the eyes that gaze far into the distance . . . His dance semaphores the signs of a distant people connected each to each in a chain that reaches back to the dawn of time. I suddenly recall Earl's late father. He was the last person who lived in the age when Inuit were true Inuit. One night in Point Hope I listened to the old man tell an ancient tale of the whale hunt.

After the rehearsal, everyone prays together. Then I hug John, Molly, Earl and other friends one by one, rejoicing in our reunion.

Night deepens. We are at the World Eskimo-Indian Olympics. Thousands fill the venue. Now at last it is Point Hope's turn to perform. Once their spirited drumming has begun, the adorable children, the elders, the women, each dances their own personal story. Then it is Earl's moment. Before a packed audience, he lets loose like a fish who has found water, unleashing a groove that plunges us into soulful rapture. When the crowd showers him with cheers and applause, I feel happy and proud as if it was for me. I'm overcome with the urge to tell someone out there, I don't care who: I paddled an *umiak* with that man to hunt whales in the Arctic Ocean.

The next day, John, Molly and Earl come to our house. Soon we are reminiscing about the whale hunt now thirteen years past.

'That quiet night when the whale came,' says John, 'I seem to recall you getting chewed out by everyone for running on the ice.'

'True,' I admit. 'How was I supposed to know that the whale might be alerted to the sound?'

I have profound respect for John, the spiritual leader of Point Hope, a village that has maintained strong traditions. I see him as something like a father and he treats me like a son. The conversation turns to my soon-to-be-born child.

'Let's give him an Inuit name right now,' John suggests.

'Really?' I say.

'Nipik. We'll make it Nipik,' Earl decides. 'That's my mother's name. I'm sure she'll be pleased.'

I recall the white-haired old woman at Point Hope, now eighty-four and as spry as ever. All that has happened is that a name has been passed on, and yet I have the distinct impression that something is connecting.

Suddenly John begins to hum an old Inuit song. It is as though he is quietly conversing with someone. With beams of warm sunlight shining in through the window, we all listen to the song.

Sitka

The most beautiful town in all of Alaska has to be Sitka. Located on Baranof Island, one of countless islands in the seas of the panhandle, it was the capital of Alaska back in the nineteenth century when the Russian Empire ruled the land to reap benefits from the fur trade. In the days when San Francisco was still a rural nowhere, Sitka became the cultural center of the entire West Coast, known as 'the Paris of the Pacific', a scenic dreamlike port city surrounded by lakes and forests holding remnants of ancient glaciers.

After the Russian Empire lost the Crimean War of 1856 to an alliance of France and Britain, it decided to relinquish ownership of Alaska, and in 1867 finally sold the entire territory along with the Aleutian Islands to the USA for a mere 7.2 million dollars. In 1906, the capital was moved to the booming Gold Rush town of Juneau and Sitka saw its star rapidly fall, receding completely from the historical stage within less than a century.

Despite this decline, however, the city holds a special attraction for me and many other Alaskans; it is a place people like us dream of living in one day. The deep coniferous forests that press along the seashore. The glacier-cradling mountains. The humpback whales raising spray from their spouts as they swim the island coves. The spectacular rain-hazed city. And finally the people, who seem to breath slowly within the rhythm of timeless nature.

While chasing whales on an August voyage through the panhandle, I decide to stop off in Sitka for the first time in a decade. I come with the names of several people who friends from the city have told me to contact and no itinerary of any sort. Thanks to my lack of planning, I chance upon the only cozy lodging run by an indigenous family in town. The proprietors are Tlingit, a proud totem-pole people who ruled this land until their defeat at the hands of Russian invaders.

The master of the house is the mother, a dignified woman just over sixty. She tells me that the lodgings are the old rooms of her children, unchanged since they moved out. A dinner party with relatives and neighbors is held at night, as the daughter Georgina happens to be visiting home with her family. A charming and beautiful woman in whom the ancient blood of the Tlingit flows, Georgina is married to a white man with whom she has a nine-year-old son. I can tell from her mother's affectionate gaze how proud she is of her daughter, who has some kind of important job related to state medical and social services for indigenous people.

The guests are served a delectable forty-five-pound king salmon fresh-caught by Georgina's son and we all enjoy an unpretentious evening together, during which I quietly watch the faces of the older folk who have lived dauntless amid majestic nature. Eventually the conversation turns to a recent incident. A man out fishing the nearby seas is said to have come upon a mountain of a whale that flung him and his small boat into the air with its tail. He purportedly landed atop the behemoth and proceeded to swim along with it while riding on its back.

The elder folk don't even raise an eyebrow at this fantastical tale, merely gazing out the window at the sea with mild expressions on their faces. A bygone era tucked away in their hearts, they also watch the children of the era to come with eyes that adhere to the movement of all things. The children in turn seem to live confidently, while a part of them looks back on the era of the elder folk as if concerned they have forgotten something precious. And yet amid the flow of time, ways of life go on changing; and, like ceaselessly moving clouds, we never return to the same form twice. Does the bittersweet warmth I feel now come from having discovered such inklings in scenes of human life?

One person a friend has told me to meet is Patty, a white woman working to carry on the knowledge of indigenous herbal medicine. She appears with a pair of old Tlingit women in tow and takes me into the woods to pick devil's club. Leading the old women along by their hands into deep forest, I immediately spot a dense clump of the pesky plant. The leaves carry numerous spines on their underside, making devils' club the ultimate nuisance when you are out hiking. But the tea made from whittling the skin of its stem is apparently the most potent of the various medicinal herbs in the region. One of the old women previously suffered from cancer for which she was issued a grim prognosis. Five years have since passed and her befuddled doctor reportedly calls her survival a miracle. She never told him about the remedies she had been taking.

While helping the old women scrape the stalks of devil's club under the darkness of the canopy, Patty explains.

'The reason for her secrecy is, you see, that these women were repeatedly told since childhood never to tell white people important things. This is no doubt because everything, from their shamanism to their language, was taken away from them by us. She' – Patty gestures toward the cancer survivor – 'says she heard a story from her father as a child about how he spotted an injured bear in the forest many years earlier that was chewing on a stalk of devil's club and smearing it on its wound. I believe that something like that may have actually happened.

'I decided I wanted to truly learn about medicinal herbs after an old indigenous woman I met when I first came to this land began to guide me. Her knowledge was astounding and she began to teach me in the indigenous way. What I mean is, she told me to listen quietly and carefully. All plants have some kind of power, and if you want to receive that power you have to approach them softly with your ears open . . .'

The following day, I visit a woman named Jamie who lives in a seaside forest twelve miles outside Sitka. She has been recommended to me for the thoroughly rugged wilderness lifestyle of her and her family.

When I arrive at the vacant and utterly silent cove, Jamie comes out to meet me on the beach. Her three-year-old son is perched alone on the rocks exposed with the retreat of the tide. Seeing the simple sturdy face of this small boy is all I need to picture just how this family lives. The father is out fishing with their fourteen-year-old son and will not be back for some time.

I struggle to square Jamie's slender figure and affability with her chosen existence, remote from human society with no electricity or running water. Just a few steps into the forest from the beach is their time-worn cabin. There are so many ways to live, I think to myself as I so often do. This is Jamie's and my first topic of conversation, though we have just met.

'Someone once said that there are two kinds of people in this world: those who live strange and interesting lives; and the other kind, who I have never met. I guess that's to say that there is nothing so fascinating in this world as each person's life.'

While Jamie describes how she and her family get on in this outlying place, she tells me: 'Sometimes when people come here, they say how much they admire this spectacular life we have in nature. But give them a week and they can't stand it. The loneliness and the isolation get to them. So is that to say that I'm free of such feelings? No way in hell. I had to face down loneliness so bad it hurts. But once I got through that, I discovered a strange kind of mental balance. If you're in the city, you can keep on running away from the loneliness inside you. You just turn on the TV or call up your friend or what have you. There are so many ways to avoid confronting it. But you can't do that here. Instead you have this mysterious peace of mind that only comes from getting past the agony of your seclusion.'

Sitka holds a special attraction for me; it is a place I dream of living in one day. The beauty of the city is no doubt thanks to the depth of the forest that stretches behind it. The people here are always listening carefully in some part of themselves to voices calling from the ancient past.

Night Flight

'Michio, this is turning into a blizzard!' says Don Ross as he emerges from the Cessna he has just landed at my campsite. 'If we don't get out of here, we'll be trapped for a week for sure. There's a big low-pressure system coming.'

We're near the mouth of the Hulahula, a river that empties into the Arctic Ocean.

'You think we can make it back to Fairbanks?' I ask. 'I don't see us getting there before night.'

I'm struggling to accept that a blizzard could be on its way. It's only August and just yesterday I was wearing a T-shirt as thousands of caribou passed through like a wave.

'Hurry up!' Don shouts. 'Ten minutes – pack up in ten!'

The tundra is suddenly shrouded in a leaden veil, whether cloud or mist there is no telling. It approaches like a moving wall. Already the Brooks Range has vanished from sight.

It's only a matter of time. We've got to take off from the tundra before the wind arrives.

Once I've folded up my tent and stuffed my heaps of gear into the small Cessna, we lift off in a hurry. In the uncannily rapid motion of the clouds, I would have recognized the telltale signs of a nearing storm even without Don's warning. I've made it out of conditions like this several times before. Not that it's the sort of thing you get used to. Make one mistake or encounter a bit of bad luck and you're done for.

To stay clear of entering the eerie shroud billowing in, Don keeps us on a flight path just above the ground. Gliding low as if to lick the undulations of the tundra, the plane crosses several valleys. Then Don gradually raises our altitude, and rain laced with sleet begins to beat on the windows. It really does seem like it's about to snow.

I'm feeling uneasy. Night is going to fall long before we reach Fairbanks. Once darkness descends, we won't be able to land no matter what problems we encounter along the way. But we've already taken off. There's nothing for me to do except leave everything to Don.

The Cessna threads gaps in the blackening clouds that swirl in ever more thickly around us. Whenever a path closes up, Don swiftly loops back and searches out another opening. As we zigzag in step to the movement of the clouds, conditions changing minute to minute, I'm left completely disoriented. Too caught up in our predicament for conversation, all we can do is stare ahead transfixed.

Through occasional breaks in the clouds, we glimpse rivers tumbling down the precipitous valleys of the Brooks Range.

Beyond the point of no return, there is no longer anywhere to land. We'll just have to cross these mountains. Don knows what he's doing, I tell myself. It'll be fine.

Many bush pilots we know have died. They flew the Alaskan wilderness on an almost a daily basis and most of them were highly skilled. If only experience and ability were a guarantee of avoiding accidents in this land. I suppose what it all comes down to is whether and when you draw that one unlucky card. Sooner or later, it's sad, but that's just how it has to go. Because the unlucky card waiting for each Alaskan bush pilot is in some way the very thing that attracts them to this land in the first place.

But some pilots can unconsciously refrain from drawing it. This has nothing to do with flight technique, nor is it quite the same thing as judgement; it's more like a subtle gift innate to the person. I suspect that Don possesses this invisible something. It may have something to do with fortune in the larger sense of that term.

After a two-hour struggle, the plane is beyond the Brooks Range. Darkness has set in around us, but we seem to be gradually veering from the cyclone, for stars have begun to appear inside rifts in the clouds. Then, around the time we cross the Yukon River, the sky completely clears and to our astonishment the heavens fill with stars. This transformation leaves us stunned even as we breath sighs of relief.

We now finally have the freedom of attention to talk. So we put on our headphones, bring the small mics to our mouths and start murmuring to each other amid the noise of the engine. My conversations with Don in the air are always wide-ranging.

Our dreams for the future. Don's memories of flying over African refugee camps. The changes Alaska is undergoing. The future of humankind . . . Such serious topics emerge now and then from what is mostly just joshing. The unreality of flying through the sky uplifts and purifies our spirits.

But tonight we have little to say. When the air currents stabilize, it turns into a quiet flight. This is my first time soaring through the night in a Cessna. Stars sparkle by the millions like a scene I seem to recall in Saint-Exupéry's *Night Flight*. With the landscape around us remaining still, it is as though we are floating in an ocean of night. The mountains, the rivers, the forests – the world fades to mere outline in the dim, recounting many meanings in its concealment like an owl calling out to us from a dark wood. Surely this is why we have few words to exchange. Life becomes abstract, primordial.

I know what Don is thinking right now, if hazily. I keep returning to what his wife told me just the other day.

'He thinks that he's going to be next . . .'

Last fall, not long after two bush pilots we know died in quick succession, another bush pilot who was our mutual friend and Don's best friend in the world lost his life. As much as I wanted to cheer Don up in his grief, I knew there was nothing I could do. As soon as winter came, he bought a little old camping car and went off on a road trip across the USA, visiting the people he missed. After his return, I could see him gradually overcoming something. But I'm certain that he is still haunted by bereavement. This unseasonable blizzard, just like the one during which our friend went missing in the Brooks Range, can't be helping. It's all right

Don, you're not going to die, I want to tell him, but it just isn't in me.

I recall a summer afternoon with Don some years ago. We were growing tired from a continuous flight over the vast Arctic tundra, on a search for the great caribou migration, and wanted to find somewhere to rest, when a swathe of pink-tinged land below suddenly captured our attention and Don arced us down to investigate.

Touching down, the Cessna bounced to a stop and we discovered the source of the vibrant hue: an ocean of flowers as far as the eye could see. The expansiveness of that space, bounded only by staggeringly distant horizons, was almost intoxicating. We decided to go for a walk and then just kept on walking. Not a caribou in sight, the only thing that greeted our eyes were tiny flowers upon flowers of the deep north, all swaying in the breeze. It was a landscape of no importance, and yet wasn't I destined to remember it at some time in the future out of a fierce longing for the past, the plains rippling in the breeze and the mysterious color of the moss clinging to the rocks, nothing remarkable but all of it settling in the depths of memory . . .?

Once we pass over the low range of the White Mountains, we see the glow of Fairbanks. Although it is a small city, to us returning from the wilds it's like the nightscape of a great radiant metropolis. The knowledge that this vista is artificial through and through doesn't reduce my pleasure at the sight. Gazing at those innumerable lights from the sky turns even the doings of humanity to abstraction and raises an overwhelming tenderness in my heart.

Valley of Ten Thousand Smokes

Once I finish climbing the hill, the entirety of the Valley of Ten Thousand Smokes spreads out before me. Evening sunbeams shine down between clouds, illuminating the immense desolate valley in mystic shades of ochre. It is a truly inhospitable landscape. With no signs of life to be found, the only movement is the constant shifting of light and shade. The deep many-channeled canyons look even more uncanny now that they are sunken into shadow, reminiscent of the surface of the moon.

I struggle to imagine the valley covered in green forests, as it had been from ancient times until the day that everything changed here. The volcano Mount Katmai looming on the horizon now pretends innocence even as it belches white smoke into the air. The transformation of this place betokens the latent power of nature that transcends human knowledge, a capricious will that reverts all things it has raised up through long effort into nothing. Does nature truly lack meaning of its own?

I set up my tent in a swathe of grass on the edge of a cliff with a fine vantage, feeling a kind of plaintive sentimentality welling slowly inside me. Could my friend T have spent his last night twenty years ago pitching tent like this? As I sit on a ground of volcanic ash and gaze at the valley under the final rays of the lingering sun, that distant summer day comes back to me as though it were only yesterday. Even this bitter memory has transformed somewhere in the kaleidoscope of passing years into something I recall wistfully.

A breeze rises. Soon the sun will slip behind the shoulder of Mount Katmai.

The Katmai National Monument is an enormous national park located in southwestern Alaska. Dotted with innumerable lakes, it becomes the world's largest trove of salmon in the summer, as the fish swim upstream to spawn in their birthplace. Although I have visited the area many times to photograph bears, this is my first excursion to the especially remote Valley of Ten Thousand Smokes. The Pacific Ring of Fire extends here from Japan along the Aleutian Islands. Due to its seismic power, no trace remains of the green vales or of the human settlements that once existed nearby.

At seven and a half thousand feet above sea level, Mount Katmai has the highest summit in the region. Nevertheless, the Inuit of Katmai village made no mention of its eruption in their legends, hardly paying the volcano any mind, likely because the peak was only just visible from the village in the northwestern sky; the rest of it was concealed by numerous layers of mountains. In any case, the villagers felt the first of the earthquakes that would set Mount Katmai off on June 1st, 1912. Ground shocks grew more intense by the day, driving an ever-greater number to flee in terror for the coast, until by the morning of June 6th the village was completely abandoned.

One of the few eyewitnesses to the eruption was a man with the superlatively silly name of American Pete. The mayor of another village called Savonoski, Pete was out hunting with friends in the wilds some eighteen miles northeast of Mount Katmai. Just as the party was clearing out camp, they were startled by a series of earthquakes. It was at around noon that day that the volcano moved.

Pete's account of what followed was subsequently recorded by an expedition to the valley led by botanist Robert Fiske Griggs.

> The Katmai mountain blew up with lots of fire and fire came down trail from Katmai with lots of smoke. We go fast Savonoski. Everybody get bidarka (skin boat). Helluva job. We come Naknek one day, dark, no could see. Hot ash fall. Work like hell.

American Pete and his hunting pals were lucky. They continued paddling down Naknek River in their *bidarkas* and managed to flee to the coastline, while a strong southern wind that happened to blow that day carried the massive quantity of erupted material in the opposite direction. Considering the size of the explosion, the fact that no one died and almost no one witnessed it is a testament to Alaska's sparsely populated immensity. The force was powerful enough to send ash up to stratospheric air currents that carried it all the way to Africa and to reduce the average temperature that year by 1.8 degrees, bringing a cool summer to the entire northern hemisphere.

Three years later in 1915, the Griggs expedition arrived, becoming the first visitors to the unrecognizably altered terrain. His objective was to investigate the condition of the area around Mount Katmai and assess the recovery of vegetation. An old sixteen-millimeter recording of the journey survives. The film shows the team approaching incrementally, wading nearly waist deep through the tremendous quantities of ash that smothered the land. When they finally mounted the last hill, the vista that greeted them was an expansive valley filled with innumerable jets of steam that rose into the air as if from countless chimneys.

Awestruck, Griggs dubbed the place Valley of Ten Thousand Smokes. In photos, you can see expedition members cooking with frying pans placed on the ground and lifting huge boulders with ease. In a single day, the valley of Katmai had gone from thick forest to something otherworldly.

The Valley of Ten Thousand Smokes that stretches in front of me now, over half a century later, is different yet again. The apocalyptic landscape has cooled and the only sound you hear is that of the wind. Still, I can conjure a clear image of what Griggs observed. While Mount Katmai maintains a semblance of tranquility, it could easily move again someday, revealing to us that the earth we stand upon with such reassurance is not as safe as it may seem.

I thinks this place has reminded me of T due to the special connection I have felt to volcanoes since the day he died in an eruption twenty years ago. You could even call the connection a sort of intimacy, as though I myself belonged among them. Whenever a volcano goes off somewhere in the world, I listen carefully for the sound.

T and I had been good friends since middle school and always shared a certain aspiration. We both had a vague dream to one day go off and see another world, a land far and unknown, inhabited by people with different values from our own, containing nature possessed of a power far surpassing even human ingenuity. We looked up to the explorers of Central Asia – Vladimir Arsenyev, Eric Shipton, Sven Hedin – enthralled most of all by the natural wonders that formed the background of their adventures: the endless expanse of the taiga, the towering mountains, the deserts.

Once we had become college students, I stepped into the world of Alaska and T into that of the highland indigenous people of the Philippines. We must have been seeking out another reality, something definite that would shake up our existence, something invisible that lay in parallel to the everyday. Perhaps we wanted to find, whether in nature or in human ways of life, a mirror to reflect ourselves back to us, a mirror thrillingly clear . . .

When T climbed the mountain in Shinshu that summer day, he was supposed to camp in a naturally formed cave just below the summit. But another climber seemed to have befouled the shelter when using it previously, so T changed plans and pitched tent after ascending to the peak. That, at least, is as far as his diary records.

Had the first tremors already begun? Did he hear a thunderous voice from the depths of the Earth? Were the birds and beasts acting strangely in anticipation of freak disaster? Who could have imagined that this mountain, dormant since the Edo period, would unleash its fire with untold force that night?

What labyrinth of time you stumbled into, though perhaps that is the very world that we had always talked about with each other. In your last moments, I wonder if you turned around, my poor departed friend, and gazed unmoving at the volcano erupting right in front of you. I can still remember the peculiar feeling I had when I learned that you would never be coming back. My sadness had no outlet for so long, until one day I forgot all about it and found myself asking you again and again what you saw that night.

After the last of the fading sunlight turns the Valley of a Thousand Smokes the color of fire for just an instant, the darkness of night slowly creeps in around me and the wind grows stronger.

Forget-Me-Nots

I am caught in an Arctic blizzard one November night when I learn that my first child has been born. The storm seems to interfere with the signal as the voice conveying the news to me comes through faintly over the radio. Once I have switched the device off, I feel a sort of excitement bubble up from deep inside me. Turning out the headlamp, I curl up in my sleeping bag. But sleep refuses to come, with the roar of the wind in my ears and thoughts churning in my head.

Sixteen years have slipped by since I began my journeys through Alaska. At some point during this period, though it's difficult to locate the precise moment, I started to think about settling down. This shift in perspective likely arose from my weariness and dissatisfaction with being always on the move. I was also becoming increasingly aware that my time in this world is finite. Whatever ultimately led me to it, my decision to put down roots brought about an immediate shift in the landscape encompassing me. Or rather, even as the landscape remained the same, nature and human ways of life grew transparent to me as though I had removed a pane of clouded glass.

No matter how deeply I penetrated the core of Alaska, I had remained a mere spectator watching incredible events play out on a screen. Then poof, it was as if my fleeting existence had become conjoined with the lifeforce of countless beings. From the great caribou herds on their grand journey through the tundra, and the humpback whales bursting into the air from the waters of the panhandle, to the Inuit and other indigenous peoples that call this land home – even the insentient mountains and rivers and winds – everything began to connect with me more intimately than ever before.

It has now been a year and a half since my wife and I married and she moved here from Japan. She has a passion for flowers, and we have encountered many varieties together on our photography expeditions to the Far North. The hardy but adorable blossoms that greet us in those wildlands truly enthrall her, and she seemed to immediately appreciate how their appearance during the brief summer brings solace after the long winter. If there was no season of darkness and the flowers of Alaska bloomed year-round, they would not soothe the human heart in quite the same way.

Thanks to her influence, I have learned to see flowers anew and am gradually beginning to experiment with photographing them for the first time. Before, my attention was always focused on the vast grandeur of the wilderness.

Now, the landscape that reveals itself only when you're bent over feels fresh to me.

Last year we visited the Aleutian Islands specifically to shoot flowers. This archipelago on the Bering Sea hosts unique ecosystems that diverge significantly from those of the mainland, likely because it never froze over in the last Ice Age. Treeless, with chill winds blasting constantly, the environment is unforgiving and bleak. Even so, the great swathes of flowers we saw there were glorious, displaying an unmistakably different kind of beauty from those that bloom in southern climes overflowing with warmth and light. For my wife, accustomed to decorating her home with the kind sold at flower shops in the city, this spectacle seemed to be something of a revelation.

What particularly impressed me on that trip were the forget-me-nots. These we began to search for the moment we stepped ashore, hoping to compare the Aleutian species to those we knew from the continent, but had little luck at first. Then, on the advice of some Aleut residents, we climbed a scree-covered slope. There too we looked everywhere without success. It wasn't until we crouched down for a moment that we spotted them right at our feet. The reason for their elusiveness then became obvious. These were not the usual blossoms we saw reaching into the breeze, but tiny inconspicuous beauties that cowered in the shadows of rocks.

'Do you know what Alaska's state flower is?' I've lost count of how many times I've asked someone this with a knowing smile. It delights me that the forget-me-not, a flower so endearing its almost tragic, represents a region that epitomizes the rugged and the rough. Not that other flowers of the deep north, seizing the momentary summer to bloom with every ounce of their strength, are any less sublime.

I can still picture the forget-me-nots arraying our campsite by the shores of the Arctic Ocean several years ago, pale-blue petals unfolding quietly in secluded hinterlands, unnoticed and unseen. This was while I was accompanying a television crew who were filming a nature documentary. Due to a combination of mishaps, the shoot wasn't going to plan and the hours just kept ticking by without progress. Soon all anyone could think about was getting the job done so they could go home. While I fully sympathized with their impatience, it seemed to me that they weren't even paying attention to the natural world around them. Amid the fraught atmosphere, I presently grew concerned and decided to speak privately with the director.

'We've done everything we can,' I tried to tell him, 'but we're dealing with nature here, so we can't expect everything to go the way we want. In ten, twenty years, no one is going to care about a slight difference in the quality of your footage. So why don't you quit thinking about work for just fifteen minutes, maybe half an hour, and acknowledge the fact that you are here and that the flowers are in bloom and that the wind is blowing and that we're camping all the way out here beside the Arctic Ocean. It's not every day that people get to come to a place like this. I think you're throwing away a special opportunity . . .'

I could almost hear the forget-me-nots saying their piece along with me as they swayed in the wind. 'We cannot exist in the past or the future, only the present.'

The scenery around our campsite was beyond incredible. A river so clear it was almost invisible flowed ever northward, as small herds of passing caribou glanced curiously in our direction. A few careful steps into the tundra revealed plover and sandpiper hens concealed in the grass atop their eggs, perched motionless until someone accidentally drew too close. They would then flutter out into the open and pretend to drag a broken wing, leading the intruder away from their young, while all the while pomarine jaegers wheeled patiently overhead, poised to swoop on abandoned nests when the chance presented itself.

I decided at one point to take a walk along the ridge that lined the river, and discovered a foxhole marked by numerous flowers in an area otherwise devoid of them. They had been fertilized by generation after generation of the inhabitants' waste. I watched for a time, until a fox pup emerged from the hole and began to frolic among the blossoms. Soon her mother appeared in the distance and dashed over carrying prey between her teeth.

Whether or not the result turns out as you anticipated, the time you spent pursuing it exists without a doubt. So what holds meaning in the end is not where you end up but the precious moments you put in trying.

The soft touch of a Far Northern breeze on my cheek, the sweet scent of summer tundra, the pale light of the midnight sun, the easy-to-miss color of tiny forget-me-nots. Standing up on impulse and focusing my awareness, I wanted to impress my sensation of the landscape in my memory. I wanted to cherish the series of moments that simply proceed without bringing anything forth. I wanted to always sense in some corner of my mind the other time that flows alongside the frantic daily exertions of humankind.

Will I be able to teach such things to my child someday? I wonder, still unable to sleep in my tent. I listen to the sound of the wind, searching for signs of a newborn life I have not yet seen in the darkness of night.

Afterword

When traveling Alaska along the rivers, you encounter a kind of scene symbolic of the land: spruce trees growing horizontally inward from the riverbanks. As a river alters its course and gradually erodes the earth over many long years, the time comes for the trees of the forest when they will stand on the bank and then slowly topple over. Especially meandering rivers etch deep banks, tilting numerous trunks and soaking many in the water. You will also spot some trees here and there that are on the verge of being washed away. I love such rugged inexorable chaotic vistas, quietly testifying to the ceaseless movement from place to place that is the providence of all things.

I still remember the day long ago, on my first trip to the shores of the Arctic Ocean, when I tried to take a photo of a dusky thrush perched on a large piece of driftwood. I was puzzled as to why the natural artifact had washed up on the edge of the Arctic tundra where trees do not grow. It turned out to be a birch that had been carried down a river on a long journey to the sea, where it rode ocean currents and at last arrived on that remote northern shore. That birch – branches gone, bark completely stripped, stretched out as if thrusting toward the heavens – was transformed almost beyond recognition. Yet it had become a part of the surround, a landmark, a spot for a dusky thrush to rest and perhaps for an Arctic fox to mark with its scent. Eventually the driftwood would decompose, giving nutrients to the soil from which a flower might one day bloom. When I considered the driftwood in this way, it began to blur the line between life and death and I perceived all things on their unending journey.

Looking back, the seventeen years since I came to this land seem to have gone by in a flash. Once the period of my travels like a rootless wandering duckweed had ended, and I had built a house and settled in Alaska, the landscape began to change for me. Now that I have gone from living alone to getting married and having a child, it has begun to show me a new aspect once again. In this book I wrote about those transitional years. Everyone is on a journey in their lives just like that birch tree. And I believe that humankind too is on a journey in the flow of a larger time.

I would like to first give my thanks to Yutaka Yukawa at Bungeishunju, who always encouraged me and who was responsible for the overall composition of this book. My sincere thanks also to everyone at the editorial department of Fukuinkan's *Mother's Friends* for allowing me to include as part of this book two years of my serialized essays.

The blossoms of fireweed have begun to open. When these are in full bloom, it is a sign that the Alaskan summer is nearing its end. In another month, the northern lights should be dancing in the night sky. The sublime autumn of the deep north is making its return again.

Michio Hoshino, July 1995

Endnotes

Wolves

p. 26, When I come here, I often recall the words of mythologist Joseph Campbell. The quote from Joseph Campbell combined several distinct passages without any indication that they were originally separate. This translation separates these quotes in deference to Campbell's texts, with the addition of connecting sentences where necessary.

p. 26, He once wrote of 'a sacred place where the walls and laws of the temporal world may dissolve to reveal a wonder.' Quote from Joseph Campbell, *The Mythic Image* (Princeton: Princeton University Press, 1984), p. 184.

p. 26, 'This is an absolute necessity . . . something eventually will happen.' Quote from Joseph Campbell, *The Power of Myth* (New York: Knopf Doubleday, 2011), p. 115.

p. 26, 'People claim the land . . . invest the land with spiritual powers.' Ibid.

p. 27, Mount Salisbury and Denali were on full display in a ring all around me. While there is a Mount Salisbury in the Elias Mountains, there are seemingly no other references to one in the vicinity of Ruth Glacier or Denali National Park, nor to any mountain with a similar pronunciation. Nevertheless, the translation remains sincere to the original.

p. 28, the voice of the sacred spirit disclosing secret wisdom. This translation follows Hoshino's original gender-neutral account of the Navajo Little Storm myth. It is unclear whether Hoshino had the Great Spirit or another metaphysical notion in mind, the direct translation 'sacred spirit' is used here in the absence of clarity.

Old Crow

p. 38, They come from communities like Arctic Village, Chalkyitsik and Venetie. Hoshino's original text names a village called 'Vitanii' but as there appears to be no such place in Alaska we can assume he meant Venetie.

From Salzburg

p. 45, A person who journeyed around Alaska over a century ago is reported to have said, 'You should never go to Alaska as a young man because you'll never be satisfied with any other place as long as you live.' The author of the quote, who Hoshino leaves unnamed, is John Muir, the 'Father of National Parks'.

p. 47, Hallstatt valley. When writing 'Hallstatt valley' Hoshino appears to be referring to Hallstatt High Valley, but his phrasing has been retained.

The Amish People

p. 49, I discovered that the closest was New Wilmington and decided to take a drive there. Hoshino writes about visiting the Amish community in 'New Wellington'. As there appears to be no such place in Pennsylvania, we can assume he meant New Wilmington – a town approximately sixty miles from Pittsburgh and home to an established Amish community since the mid-1800s.

On Naoyuki Sakamoto

The original essay contains several place names and other details that would be unfamiliar to many readers. This translation therefore weaves in some minor contextual information, including locations and dates, to help readers better follow the text.

p. 59, *Footprints in Snowfields*. The quotes Hoshino uses in this essay are from Sakamoto Naoyuki, *Setsugen no ashiato* (Footprints in snowfields) (Tokyo: Meikeidō, 1965) p. 39–68, 188–209.

Ocean Currents

As with 'On Naoyuki Sakamoto', the original essay contains several obscure details, and this translation weaves in some minor contextual additions for the benefit of readers.

p. 78, SS *Baychimo*. SS *Baychimo* was built in 1914 and was a trading vessel, not a whaler as Hoshino reports his friend Dee suggesting. It was indeed one of the ghost ships seen along the Alaska coast, however, having been abandoned in 1931 and sighted several times between then and 1969.

Midnight Sun

p. 95, I have followed the roaming caribou as though guided down a time tunnel. 'Time tunnel'"may refer to the 1966 live action science fiction TV show, *Time Tunnel*, which aired in Japan on NHK in 1967, when Hoshino would have been the right age to have watched it. However, Hoshino does not indicate that it is a title, so I have chosen not to capitalize the term.

Ruth Glacier

p. 105–106, They say that it is from tens of thousands to hundreds of millions of years ago and has only just arrived. Hoshino overestimates the age of the starlight visible to the naked eye. However, this does not affect his poetic insight about the night sky and the translation remains sincere to the original.

In Search of Totem Poles

p. 117, This was approximately eighteen thousand years ago. On page 46, Hoshino writes 'ten thousand years ago'. Current estimates of the of date of initial migration to the Americas range widely.

p. 121, Evidence of human settlement on this island is said to go back seven thousand years. Recent evidence suggests that there was human presence on Haida Gwaii approximately thirteen thousand years ago – six thousand years earlier than Hoshino indicates.

Lituya Bay

p. 130, The book also records the following account, from renowned mountaineer and cartographer Bradford Washburn. All quotes concerning Jim Huscroft are from Dave Bohn's *Glacier Bay: The Land and the Silence* (San Francisco: Sierra Club, 1967), pp. 31–32. They appear in a lengthy account provided by Robert Bates, a man affiliated with the American Alpine Club. Hoshino misattributes this account to Bradford Washburn.

p. 133, And his death would not mark the end of the chronicle of Lituya Bay. Although Hoshino does not make this clear, his summary of the Tlingit legend and the story of the tsunami that struck Lituya Bay is largely borrowed from *Glacier Bay: The Land and the Silence*.

Kiska

p. 140, 'Now I understand why . . . We simply refuse to come to terms with it.' Quoted text is from an interview with Dorothy Brannon, the widow of US military Charles E Brannon, in Sawachi Hisae, *Umi yo nemure middowē – kaisen no sei to shi* (O ocean sleep thee well: the living and the dead of the Battle of Midway*)* (Tokyo: Bungeishunju, 1987), p. 205. She spoke in English, but it was not practicable to obtain the original interview text, so her words were back translated.

Death of a Bush Pilot

p. 145, Roger Dowding has died in a plane crash. The original seems to refer to 'Roger Darwin'; however, I translated this as 'Roger Dowding', as this is the correct name of the deceased. The man referred to as 'Jim Jones' could not be definitively identified, so the name was transcribed as is.

p. 147–148, 'The pilot flew low over the river . . . But this guy, he's a real pilot.' Quote from Kim Heacox and Fred Hirschmann, *Bush Pilots of Alaska* (Berkeley: Graphic Arts Center Publishing, 1989), p. 18.

The Traveling Tree

p. 154, *Animals of the North*. William O Pruitt, *Animals of the North* (New York: Harper & Row, 1967).

Inborn River

p. 172, When I turn onto Cloudberry Lane. Hoshino appears to write
'Crowberry Road' but there does not seem to be any such place in
the vicinity of Fairbanks, whereas Nancy and Bill Fuller did in fact
spend time on Cloudberry, which, moreover, closely matches the
description in the essay.

**p. 174, Even if I knew that tomorrow the world would go to pieces,
I would still plant my apple tree today.** The quote about planting
an apple tree is often attributed to Martin Luther.

People of the Beaver

**p. 183, Athabascans, who inhabit the interior, and Inuit, who
inhabit the coasts.** Hoshino roughly divides the indigenous
peoples of Alaska into two groups, in accordance with the common
understanding at the time he was writing. However, according
to the Alaska Federation of Natives, there are eleven cultures
associated with different geographical regions: 'Eyak, Tlingit,
Haida, Tsimshian peoples live in the Southeast; the Inupiaq and
St. Lawrence Island Yupik live in the north and northwest parts
of Alaska; Yup'ik and Cup'ik Alaska Natives live in southwest
Alaska; the Athabascan peoples live in Alaska's interior; and
south-central Alaska and the Aleutian Islands are the home
of the Alutiiq (Sugpiaq) and Unangax peoples.' From https://
nativefederation.org/alaska-native-peoples, accessed September
22nd, 2025 9:18 am JST.

**p. 183–184, '. . .Since the distant past . . . survival and people
obeyed.'** Hoshino appears to be directly quoting David Salmon, as
Salmon has been recorded elsewhere identifying as a 'slave Indian'
and describing his wife as a 'Best Indian.' For example, see https://
www.tananachiefs.org/about/our-leadership/traditional-chiefs/
chief-david-salmon/my-father-saved-my-life/, accessed September
22nd, 2025 9:48 am JST.

p. 186, I recall a passage from a book I once read. The quote is taken
from Tanigawa Gan, *Monogatari kōkyō* (Symphony of story) (Tokyo:
Chikuma Shobō, 1982) pp. 112–113.

Sitka

p. 206, Saint-Exupéry's *Night Flight*. Antoine de Saint-Exupéry, *Night Flight* (London: Harmsworth, 1932).

Valley of Ten Thousand Smokes

p. 210, The Katmai National Monument is an enormous national park located in southwestern Alaska. Although the Katmai National Monument was officially renamed Katmai National Park and Preserve in 1980, the translation follows Hoshino in using the former name.

p. 211, In any case, the villagers felt the first of the earthquakes that would set Mount Katmai off on June 1st, 1912. Mount Katmai was initially thought to be the source of the eruption in 1912, but it was later determined to be Novarupta, approximately six miles away.

p. 211, 'The Katmai mountain blew up . . . Hot ash fall. Work like hell.' Quote taken from *Witness: Firsthand Accounts of the Largest Volcanic Eruption in the Twentieth Century,* published by the Katmai National Park and Preserve's National Park Service. Found at https://npshistory.com/publications/katm/witness.pdf. Accessed August 28th, 2025, 9:27 am JST.

Translator's Acknowledgments

Michio Hoshino will always hold a special place in my heart because he was the first author I tried to read in Japanese. Tried to read because I was an undergraduate student still completing my first year of Japanese study, and I was not yet fully capable of understanding his writing. He was also the first author who elicited in my the burning desire to translate a book. That book was *The Traveling Tree*. In other words, the collection of essays you are currently reading was the point of departure for my career as a literary translator and perhaps also as a bilingual author.

More than 16 years have already passed since, like Hoshino, I moved from the home of my birth and rearing to a distant land –though Hoshino and I traveled in opposite directions across the Pacific, him away from Japan and me toward it. While I would have been delighted to translate this wonderful book earlier on in my journey, I think it is fitting that I have ultimately done so now, as I am the same age as Hoshino when he began to write the essays included, and I resonate more than ever with his insights on life and the passage of time.

I am grateful to everyone who believed in this translation and read bits and pieces of it over the years, including Matt Treyvaud, Louise Heal Kawai, Alison Watts, Dreux Richard and Minako Ichihashi. A special thanks to my Tokyo homestay mother, Aya Kikuchi, for introducing me to Hoshino's work when I was a student, to Saho Baldwin and Hiroshi Arai at Bungeishunju for getting behind my translation, and to the acquiring editor Jessica Minocha for recognizing the value in a commercially unconventional book of travel writing about the USA by someone from Asia.

May readers in the anglophone world come to cherish this book as much as they already do in Japan.

About the Author

Michio Hoshino (1952–1996) was a Japanese photographer and essayist who took Alaska as his lifelong subject. Born in 1952 in Ichikawa, a suburb of Tokyo, he was stricken with wanderlust and a fascination with the North from a young age. At the age of 16, in an era when a teenager leaving Japan on their own was all but unthinkable, he begged his salaryman father for travel money and stowed aboard a trans-Pacific liner to hitchhike North America alone for two months. But his introduction to Alaska did not come until he was a college student, when he became so enchanted by an aerial photograph of the Arctic village of Shishmaref that he wrote a letter to the mayor and was invited to live with an Inuit family for the summer. After graduation from Keio University and a period of mentorship under photographer Kojo Tanaka, he moved to Fairbanks to study wildlife management at the University of Alaska. The city then became his home base while he traveled Alaska and worked as a photographer for the remainder of his life. His photographs were published in magazines such as *National Geographic* and *Audobon*, in addition to many prominent Japanese publications, to which he also frequently contributed essays. *The Traveling Tree* is a bestselling collection of some of his finest writing. The book was published at the peak of Hoshino's artistic prowess, only two years before his career was tragically cut short at the age of 43 by a fatal bear attack while on a photoshoot in the Kamchatka Peninsula. He is survived by his wife and son, who have worked to spread and protect his creative legacy.

About the Translator

Eli K. P. William has spent his entire adult life in Japan making a career out of story and language. He is the author of *The Jubilee Cycle* trilogy, set in a future Tokyo, and a translator of Japanese literature, including the Yomiuri Prize winning novel *A Man* by Keiichiro Hirano. He also works as a bilingual writing consultant for a major video game development studio and recently penned his first work of fiction in the Japanese language, a short story titled *Photo Bomber*, for an anthology released by one of Japan's largest publishers. His writings and translations have appeared in such publications as *Aeon*, *Granta*, *Writer's Digest* and *Subaru*. Born and raised in Toronto, he visited Tokyo for the first time as a university student and decided to move there upon graduation. After ten years in the thick of the metropolis, he now lives in the nearby green hills with his wife and daughter. To learn more, visit https://elikpwilliam.com.